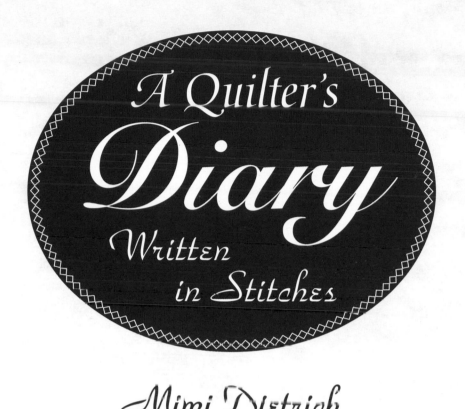

A Quilter's Diary
Written in Stitches

Mimi Dietrich

Martingale®
& COMPANY

Dedication

To my granddaughter, Julia

A Quilter's Diary: Written in Stitches
© 2008 by Mimi Dietrich

& C O M P A N Y

That Patchwork Place

That Patchwork Place® is an imprint
of Martingale & Company®.

Martingale & Company
20205 144th Ave. NE
Woodinville, WA 98072-8478 USA
www.martingale-pub.com

Credits

President & CEO ❧ Tom Wierzbicki
Publisher ❧ Jane Hamada
Editorial Director ❧ Mary V. Green
Managing Editor ❧ Tina Cook
Technical Editor ❧ Laurie Baker
Copy Editor ❧ Melissa Bryan
Design Director ❧ Stan Green
Production Manager ❧ Regina Girard
Illustrator ❧ Laurel Strand
Cover & Text Designer ❧ Regina Girard
Photographer ❧ Brent Kane

Printed in China
13 12 11 10 09 08   8 7 6 5 4 3 2 1

Library of Congress Cataloging-in-Publication Data is available upon request.

ISBN: 978-1-56477-792-8

Mission Statement

Dedicated to providing quality products and service to inspire creativity.

Contents

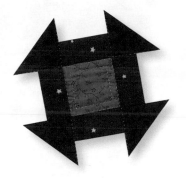

"Mimi Dietrich's Diary Quilt" by Mimi Dietrich.
The author used her favorite fabrics to tell her story.

Introduction

When I was growing up, I slept under a quilt made by my great-grandmother. I never knew her, but I always experienced a wonderful feeling when I touched that quilt. I knew that she also touched those fabrics, she stitched them together by hand, and she would have incredible stories to tell me if I could meet her today. I'd love to know more about her. Why did she make quilts? Why did she choose those fabrics? What was she thinking when she stitched? I wish she had written a diary.

I live in Baltimore, Maryland, and I love the album quilts that were originally made in my hometown in the mid-1800s. These quilts contain a variety of appliquéd blocks, each one different, like the photos in an album. Sometimes they tell a story or commemorate an event. Research has helped us decipher some of the clues and understand life during the time the quilts were made, but because the quiltmakers are no longer here to tell us about the quilts, there still are some secrets in the stitches. I'd love to know more about those quiltmakers. I wish they had written diaries about their quilts.

Many of us are blocked by the words journal, history, and diary because we don't like to write or we feel intimidated by the process. But we are all quilters—we love to quilt! What if we stitched our stories into Diary quilts and let the quilt blocks speak for us?

The idea for making Diary quilts began even before I realized it. When I first started quilting I was fascinated by the wide variety of traditional quilt patterns and their names. I made a sampler quilt with a Churn Dash, Log Cabin, Rail Fence, Bow Tie, Dresden Plate, and Grandmother's Flower Garden block. I learned to piece and appliqué using a variety of quilting techniques. I love these traditional designs and the heritage they represent. As I was stitching that sampler quilt, I remember thinking how much fun it would be to make a quilt in which all the blocks were personally meaningful to my life.

However, as the saga of everyday living continued to unfold, that idea got lost in the shuffle. Over the last 30 years, young children kept me busy, and then a career in quilting, writing, and teaching kept me focused on specific projects. But when my granddaughter was born, the need to tell my tale became even stronger. I wanted to make a quilt to give her so I could tell my story. I wanted her to know about my life. I wanted to make an heirloom legacy quilt for her, a diary in stitches!

Finally, that little seed of an idea that was planted years ago began to germinate. I pulled together all my thoughts about my life, researched traditional blocks and their names, and picked the ones that fit my story. I love to appliqué, so I designed additional blocks that represented parts of my life. And then I made my Diary quilt.

This was such a wonderful, meaningful experience for me that I wanted other quilters to tell their stories in stitches, too. With help from a group of quilting friends, I'm able to share the ideas, inspirations, and memories presented in this book to help you make your own Diary quilt. Whether you like to quilt by hand or machine, I hope you enjoy telling your story with your stitches!

Mimi Dietrich

The Making of a Diary Quilt

This section will give you some insight into how I came up with the blocks to include in my Diary quilt, and the information will ultimately help you tell your own story in fabric. What you choose to include in your own Diary quilt is completely up to you—you may find it in this book or from another source—but hopefully, you'll find inspiration along the way to help you put your own story into stitches. When you're ready to make your own Diary quilt, turn to "Getting Started" on page 11.

Gathering the Threads of Life

Take a look at the table of contents on page 3. You'll notice that the section after "Getting Started" is titled "The Threads of Life." There are many threads, or themes, that stitch our lives together. I developed the themes with a group of quilters by asking them to think about their lives in 5- or 10-year increments. For each increment, I asked them to write one important memory. There were childhood memories of playgrounds, sisters, teachers, and games; teenage memories of boyfriends (these were the most fun!), school, and friends; young adult memories of weddings, children, families, and careers; and "more mature" memories of travel, hobbies, grandchildren, and heartache.

Inspired by those memories, I asked them to think of quilt blocks that would illustrate those experiences. We talked about Grandmother's Favorite (some students just knew they were the favorite!), Friendship Star for our best friends, and Crazy Quilt for our lives. We thought about stitching blocks with secret meanings: Square Dance for a favorite dancing partner, Trip Around the World to remember a wild college adventure, and First Love for a teenage heartthrob. One student dressed Sunbonnet Sue as a nun and we relived her adventures in Catholic school. We shared our stories, laughter, and tears, and then stitched them into blocks in our quilts.

Some quilters made quilts to tell their personal stories. Others made quilts to share their stories with grandchildren. Some made diaries of their quilting life, using blocks they had made in other quilts. Some made quilts to tell another person's story—for wedding, birthday, and graduation presents.

One of my students said, "I'm making this quilt for my boys. They might not 'get it,' but I want to do it to tell them my story." Young people aren't always interested in their mom's life, but someday they will realize that this quilt is a treasure.

As you look through the categories in "The Threads of Life," I hope that the themes speak to you and help you remember wonderful experiences that you can sew together into your Diary quilt. I've provided some questions at the beginning of each thread to help spark some memories. There's also space to write your story or the reasons you are choosing a particular block—that's the "key" to your Diary quilt.

Thoughts behind the Blocks

Think of your Diary quilt as a quiltmaking adventure. Select quilt blocks that have special meaning for you, do some research to find other blocks, or design your own personal blocks!

All the blocks in this book finish to 6" square, so even a quilt with 25 blocks is easy to accomplish. Some of the patchwork blocks I found, such as Storm at Sea, were larger and had more pieces, so I simplified them using elements from the original block. You may also notice that similar blocks have different names. The names often change in regions of the country or because they have different color arrangements.

I included appliqué blocks because they are my favorites. I love to "draw" pictures with the fabric pieces. If you love to appliqué and want to design your own blocks, you can photocopy or trace images. You can even reduce a larger pattern to fit in a 6" square.

There are many more blocks in the "quilt world" than I've given you in this book, and you can, of course, add any block that you wish. You probably have a favorite block that you want to include in your quilt, and by all means you should do so.

Say It with Fabric

The fabrics you choose for your Diary quilt are also part of your story. Scraps from your clothing or quilting projects are very personal and tell something about your life. If you love traditional quilts, choose reproduction fabrics or authentic antique fabrics. Choose fabrics from the 1930s if they are your favorites (or if you were born in the '30s!). Use soft pastels, hand-dyed pieces, or bright funky fabrics to express your personality. Find a fabric you love for the border and collect coordinating fabrics for the blocks. Choose fabrics for your quilt that reflect your favorite colors or quilting experiences.

Do you love antique fabrics? Do you love bright fabrics, jewel tones, or batiks? Do you have a special collection? Do you always use a "signature" fabric? Include fabrics that are a part of you.

Your favorite multicolored fabric might be perfect for the border of your quilt and inspire the palette of colors for your Diary quilt. Look at the selvage of the fabric for the color dots that are used for printing the fabric. These dots will give you ideas for colors and help you shop for companion fabrics to use with your "inspiration" fabric.

Use specialty fabrics or conversation prints for some of the themes in the book. Look at the blocks My First Quilt Block on page 81, Handy Andy on page 24, and Granddad's Plaids on page 29. Choose fabrics printed with your favorite things in the patchwork pieces—animals, sailboats, cars, or chocolate chip cookies! You can even use vintage fabrics, old neckties, pieces from childhood clothing, or a piece of your wedding gown! The fabrics will help tell your story.

How much fabric do you need for your Diary quilt? Each quilt is different, but I suggest that you purchase two yards of your "inspiration" fabric and at least a yard of background fabric (based on approximately 25 blocks). Add fat quarters and scraps of fabrics that "play well together." Borrow fabrics from a friend, buy pieces as you travel, or add new pieces to your collection, as needed. And don't forget to check your stash! You bought those fabrics for a reason, and now might be the time to use them.

Life's Little Extras

Imagine the personal mementos you can add to your Diary quilt. Do you still have your Girl Scout badges? Did you save some buttons from a favorite dress? Do you have charms from an old charm bracelet? How about your quilt guild pin? Let them help you tell your story.

If you love quotes or poetry and want to design a block, print the words on your computer, arrange them in a 6" square, and trace them for embroidery. Below are a few simple stitches that I've used for some of the blocks in this book and that you can use to stitch your own words or pictures. I usually use two strands of embroidery floss and a size 8 embroidery needle. If you don't want to embroider the blocks, you can trace the words with a fine-point permanent pen. You could even use crayons! Remember to follow the manufacturer's instructions to iron the inked or crayoned parts to set the colors.

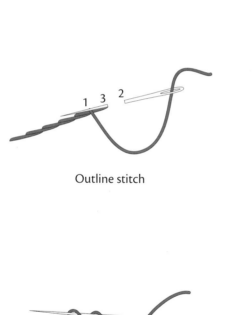

Outline stitch

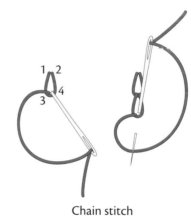

Chain stitch

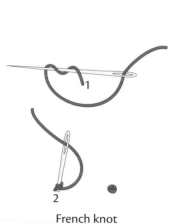

French knot

Lazy daisy stitch

Putting Your Life in Order

Each Diary quilt is different because each one is uniquely personal. Here are some suggestions for arranging anywhere from 4 to 25 blocks in either straight or on-point settings. Refer to the quilt photos in the gallery (page 104) for more ideas.

Many quilters feel that using a 1"-wide sashing strip between blocks sets each block apart and gives each block its own special space. Use a 4"- to 5"-wide border around the quilt.

Most of the patchwork blocks work well on point, especially the baskets, hearts, and flower buds. If you want to stitch the appliquéd blocks on point, you need to make that decision at the beginning of your project. When tracing the appliquéd blocks, refer to "Cutting and Marking the Background Fabric" on page 118 so that the designs will face the right direction when the blocks are stitched together.

Straight settings

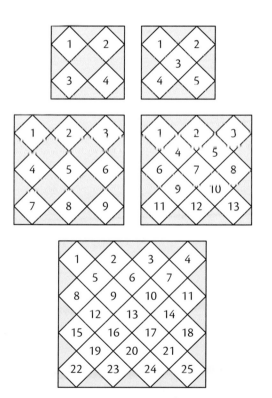

On-point settings

"Grammy's Diary Quilt" by Mimi Dietrich.
The author made this version of her diary quilt for
her granddaughter, Julia, whose favorite color is pink.

Getting Started

Oh my, there are so many decisions to make! Take a deep breath and let's get started.

Begin by dividing your life into 5- to 10-year increments, just like I had my quilting friends do. Write the ages on a piece of paper and then quickly list your strongest memories for those years. If you can't think of something, don't worry. You'll find memory-sparking questions for each thread.

Now, get a package of sticky notes and browse through the book. When you see a block that really appeals to you, reminds you of one of the memories you listed, or sparks a memory you'd forgotten about, place a sticky note on the pattern. When I did this, I was surprised that I marked only 28 blocks. I wanted 25 for my quilt, so I only had to make three big decisions! If you have too many blocks, that's OK—you might change your mind as you make your quilt, or you might decide to make your quilt larger. You can always use a block for your signature on the back. If you don't have enough blocks, get a cup of coffee and browse again!

Once you have selected your favorites, photocopy or scan the illustration of each block, enlarging each one to 450% to make it 6" square. Cut them out. Place them on a design wall or table and use them to "audition" the design of your quilt. Look at the setting suggestions on page 9 and arrange your blocks in a straight or diagonal setting. Use your favorite block in the center of the quilt, balance similar blocks opposite each other in the quilt plan, and place blocks with words near the center or in the corners. Your quilt will really start to shape up-because the blocks have meaning in your life!

Making the blocks is the next step. Choose the most meaningful ones, or the easiest ones, to start with. I started with the Holly block because I didn't have to make any big decisions. I knew exactly what colors to use! Once I got started, I didn't want to stop. Make a few blocks at a time and enjoy the memories as you think about the reason you are making each block. Keep the finished blocks together in a safe place—a cute tin box or a resealable plastic bag.

When you have several blocks, pin them to your design wall or lay them out on a table. As you add more blocks, balance the block designs and colors. To help, ask yourself a few questions: Do the fabrics, colors, and designs capture your memories? Are the block designs balanced in your quilt? Is your favorite block in the center? Are the colors balanced throughout—is there too much of any one color in any one spot? Do you need to repeat some colors in the next few blocks you make? Take a photo of your finished blocks. A small image will help you decide if you like the choices you've made for your quilt.

— Using the Cutting Charts —

Below is a key to the rotary-cutting symbols used throughout this book. For more information, see "Rotary Cutting" on page 116.

☐	Square
▭	Rectangle
◲	Square cut once diagonally to make half-square triangles
⊠	Square cut twice diagonally to make quarter-square triangles
◱	Square used for corner-square triangles

Once upon a Time

Notes from Mimi's Journal

What a great way to begin your Diary quilt!
Life is a fairy tale—with its adventures,
fairy godmothers, princes, surprises,
villains, and happy endings! Tell your
story by stitching your memories!

Inspiration

- ❧ Were fairy tales a fond part of your childhood?
- ❧ Do you love to tell stories?
- ❧ Have you researched your genealogy to find out your family story?
- ❧ Can you ask a family member about your family history?

Key to My Diary

I made this block for my Diary quilt because . . .

- -

- -

- -

Center

Refer to page 8 to chain stitch the words. You can also trace the
words with a fine-point permanent pen—or crayons!

Heritage

Notes from Mimi's Journal

I live in Baltimore, Maryland, a wonderful city that celebrates the diversity of the many people who live here. Of course, their families originally came to the United States from other countries. In the summer, festivals filled with crafts, dances, and great food keep their heritage alive.

Inspiration

- Research your genealogy; if possible, ask your parents about their parents.

- If your heritage flag has three stripes, the Flag block is wonderful to include in your quilt.

- Do you celebrate your family's heritage in a special way?

- Do certain colors remind you of the country of your heritage?

- Do you feel ties to a specific region of the United States? Are you a "Yankee" or a "Southern Belle"?

Key to My Diary

I made this block for my Diary quilt because . . .

Irish Shamrocks

1

Center

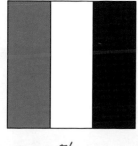

Flag

Yankee
Puzzle

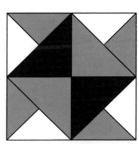

Southern Belle

Flag

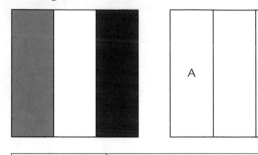
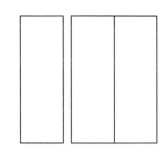

	A: Cut 1 ▭ , 2½" x 6½", from *each*

Yankee Puzzle

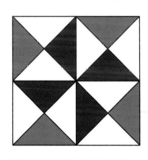

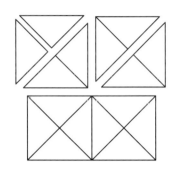

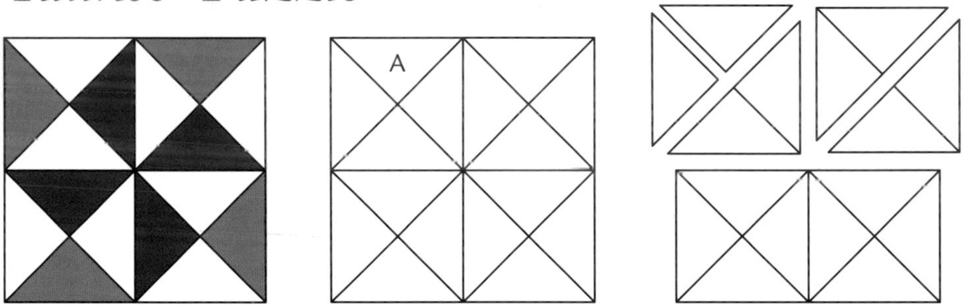

☐	A: Cut 2 ⊠ , 4¼" x 4¼"
■ ■	A: Cut 1 ⊠ , 4¼" x 4¼", from *each*

Southern Belle

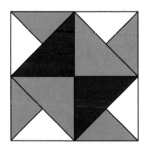
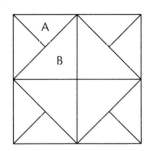
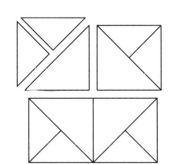

☐	A: Cut 1 ⊠ , 4¼" x 4¼"
■	B: Cut 1 ◨ , 3⅞" x 3⅞"
■	A: Cut 1 ⊠ , 4¼" x 4¼" B: Cut 1 ◨ , 3⅞" x 3⅞"

Castles in Spain

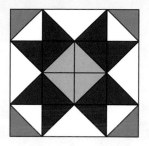 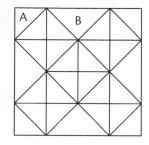 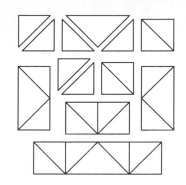

⬜	**A:** Cut 2 ◺, 2⅜" x 2⅜"	**B:** Cut 1 ⊠, 4¼" x 4¼"	
⬛	**A:** Cut 6 ◺, 2⅜" x 2⅜"		
🟦 🟦	**A:** Cut 2 ◺, 2⅜" x 2⅜", from *each*		

Dutchman's Puzzle

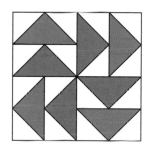 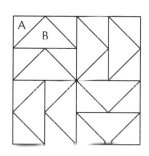 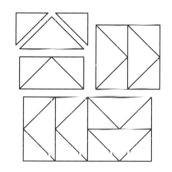

⬜	**A:** Cut 8 ◺, 2⅜" x 2⅜"
🟦 🟦	**B:** Cut 1 ⊠, 4¼" x 4¼", from *each*

Greek Cross

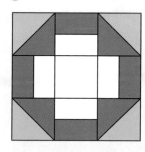 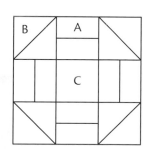 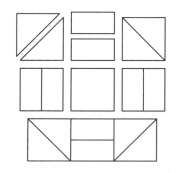

⬜	**A:** Cut 4 ▭, 1½" x 2½"	**C:** Cut 1 ⬜, 2½" x 2½"	
⬛	**A:** Cut 4 ▭, 1½" x 2½"	**B:** Cut 2 ◺, 2⅞" x 2⅞"	
🟦	**B:** Cut 2 ◺, 2⅞" x 2⅞"		

Childhood

Notes from Mimi's Journal

Back-to-school time always included a new box of 8 crayons, but when I got a big box of 64 crayons in the summertime, it was a special treat. I had to make the Crayon Box block for my quilt. My favorite color was burnt sienna—what's yours?

Inspiration

- Stitch Sunbonnet Sue in your favorite colors.
- Dress her in a piece of fabric from one of your childhood dresses.
- Make a Sister's Choice block for your sister using her favorite colors.
- Do you have fond childhood memories of playgrounds— the swings, monkey bars, or seesaw?
- Remember your high school or college with a School Colors block made in your alma mater's colors.

Key to My Diary

I made this block for my Diary quilt because . . .

- -

- -

- -

Sunbonnet Sue

Refer to page 8 to embroider lazy daisy stitches for the
flower petals. Make a French knot in the center of each flower.

Sister's Choice

School Colors Star

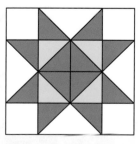

Crayon Box

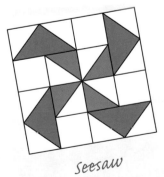

Seesaw

Seesaw

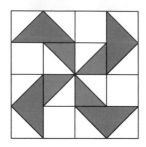 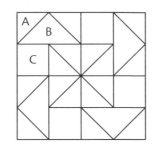 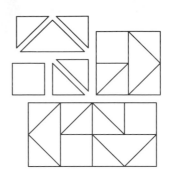

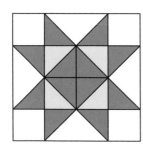 white square	**A:** Cut 6 ◺, 2⅜" x 2⅜"	**C:** Cut 4 ▢, 2" x 2"	
gray square	**A:** Cut 2 ◺, 2⅜" x 2⅜"		
gray square	**B:** Cut 1 ⊠, 4¼" x 4¼"		

Sister's Choice

 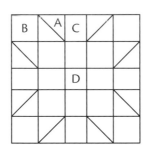 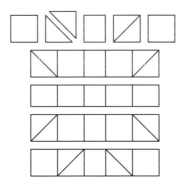

white square	**A:** Cut 4 ◺, 2⅛" x 2⅛"	**B:** Cut 4 ▢, 1¾" x 1¾"		
black square	**A:** Cut 4 ◺, 2⅛" x 2⅛"	**C:** Cut 4 ▭, 1½" x 1¾"		
gray square	**B:** Cut 4 ▢, 1¾" x 1¾"	**C:** Cut 4 ▭, 1½" x 1¾"	**D:** Cut 1 ▢, 1½" x 1½"	

School Colors Star

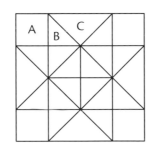 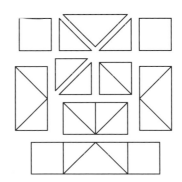

white square	**A:** Cut 4 ▢, 2" x 2"	**C:** Cut 1 ⊠, 4¼" x 4¼"	
gray square	**B:** Cut 6 ◺, 2⅜" x 2⅜"		
light square	**B:** Cut 2 ◺, 2⅜" x 2⅜"		

Schoolgirl's Puzzle

 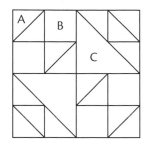 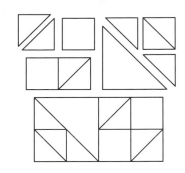

⬜	**A:** Cut 5 ◺, 2⅜" x 2⅜"		**B:** Cut 4 ☐, 2" x 2"	
⬛	**C:** Cut 1 ◺, 3⅞" x 3⅞"			
🟫	**A:** Cut 3 ◺, 2⅜" x 2⅜"			

Crayon Box

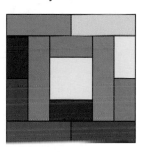 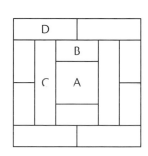 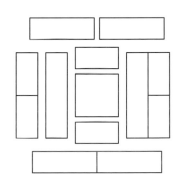

Assorted colors	**A:** Cut 1 ☐, 2½" x 2½"	**B:** Cut 6 ☐ total, 1½" x 2½"
	C: Cut 2 ☐ total, 1½" x 4½"	**D:** Cut 4 ☐ total, 1½" x 3½"

Kindergarten

 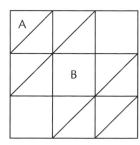 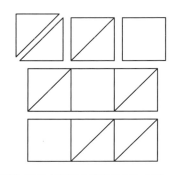

⬜	**A:** Cut 3 ◺, 2⅞" x 2⅞"		**B:** Cut 3 ☐, 2½" x 2½"	
⬛	**A:** Cut 3 ◺, 2⅞" x 2⅞"			

Parents

Notes from Mimi's Journal

Beautiful flowers grew in our backyard garden in the summertime. I don't remember Mom ever planting flowers—they just grew magically. Her favorites were the roses and she loved to bring them into the house and arrange them. Dad wore ties to work everyday, but we knew it was a special occasion when he tied his own bow tie.

Inspiration

- Did your mother or father have a special collection?

- Do you have some scraps from your dad's plaid shirts?

- Was your dad a "Handy Andy," fixing everything in the house?

- Did you always feel that you were your "Mother's Choice" or "Father's Choice"?

- Now that you are grown, do you admire your parents for their "Patience"?

Key to My Diary

I made this block for my Diary quilt because . . .

- -

- -

- -

Handy Andy

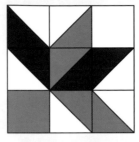

Mother's Choice

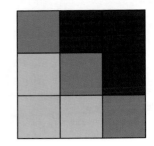

Patience

Mother's Roses

Daddy's Ties

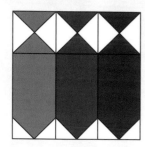 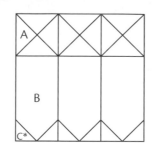 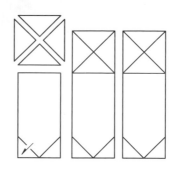

⬜	A: Cut 2 ⊠, 3¼" x 3¼" (2 left over)	C: Cut 6 ◹, 1½" x 1½"*	
🟥🟥🟥	A: Cut 1 ⊠, 3¼" x 3¼", from *each* (2 left over of *each* color)	B: Cut 1 ▭, 2½" x 4½", from *each*	

Refer to page 117 to place C squares in corners of B rectangles and sew on the diagonal line to form small triangles.

Father's Choice

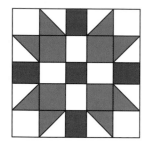 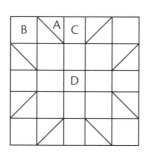 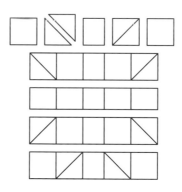

⬜	A: Cut 4 ◺, 2⅛" x 2⅛"	B: Cut 4 ☐, 1¾" x 1¾"	C: Cut 4 ▭, 1½" x 1¾"		
🟥	A: Cut 4 ◺, 2⅛" x 2⅛"	B: Cut 4 ☐, 1¾" x 1¾"			
⬛	C: Cut 4 ▭, 1½" x 1¾"	D: Cut 1 ☐, 1½" x 1½"			

Handy Andy (aka Dad's Plaids)

 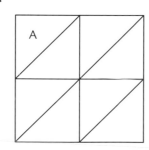 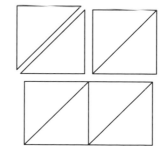

⬜	A: Cut 2 ◺, 3⅞" x 3⅞"
4 different plaids	A: Cut 1 ◺, 3⅞" x 3⅞", from *each* (1 left over of *each* color)

Mother's Choice

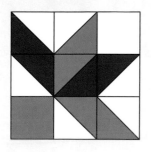 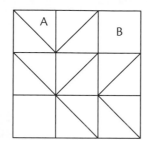 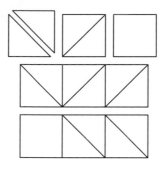

		A: Cut 3 ◺, 2⅞" x 2⅞"	B: Cut 1 ☐, 2½" x 2½"
		A: Cut 2 ◺, 2⅞" x 2⅞"	
		A: Cut 2 ◺, 2⅞" x 2⅞"	B: Cut 1 ☐, 2½" x 2½"

Mama's Teacup

 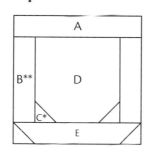 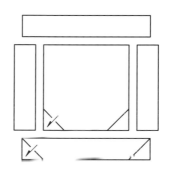

		A: Cut 1 ▭, 1½" x 6½"	B: Cut 2 ▭, 1½" x 4½"**	C: Cut 4 ◹, 1½" x 1½"*
		D: Cut 1 ☐, 4½" x 4½"	E: Cut 1 ▭, 1½" x 6½"	

*Refer to page 117 to place C squares in corners of D square and E rectangle and sew on the diagonal line to form small triangles.

**Refer to page 8 to chain stitch the teacup handle on right-hand B piece after block is completed.

Patience

 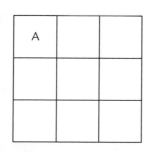 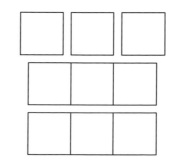

			A: Cut 3 ☐, 2½" x 2½", from *each*

Grandparents

Notes from Mimi's Journal

My great-grandmother made a Grandmother's Flower Garden quilt. I love to look at the beautiful fabrics from the 1930s and think about her sewing the pieces together by hand. Many of my students chose to piece the Grandmother's Favorite block for their quilts because they were sure that they were the family favorite— what a lovely memory!

Inspiration

- ❧ Do you have a special memory about your grandparents?
- ❧ Did your grandmother sew or quilt?
- ❧ Did your grandmother have a "Flower Garden"?
- ❧ Did your Grandfather wear plaid shirts or bow ties?
- ❧ Are you your "Grandmother's Favorite"?

Key to My Diary

I made this block for my Diary quilt because . . .

- -

- -

- -

Grandmother's Flower Garden

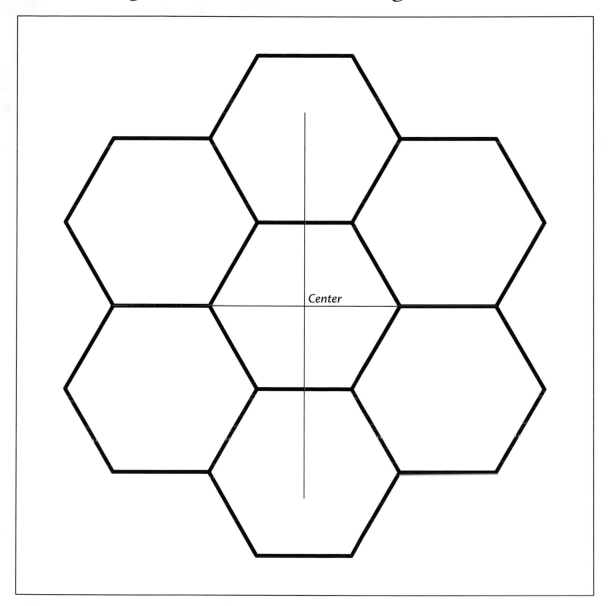

Center

Use the pattern to cut seven hexagon shapes from freezer paper. Baste the fabric to the shapes and then hand stitch them together. Appliqué the pieced unit to the center of the background square.

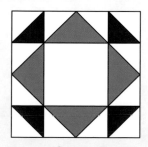

Grandmother's
Favorite

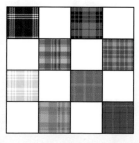

Granddad's Plaids

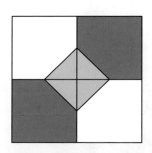

Pop-Pop's Bow Tie

Grandmother's Favorite

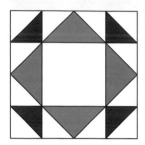 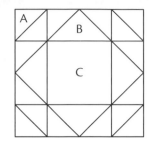 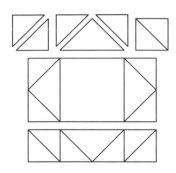

	A: Cut 6 ◺, 2⅜" x 2⅜"	**C:** Cut 1 ☐, 3½" x 3½"
	B: Cut 1 ⊠, 4¼" x 4¼"	
	A: Cut 2 ◺, 2⅜" x 2⅜"	

Grandmother's Choice

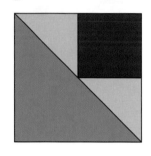 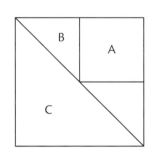 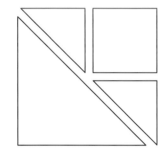

	A: Cut 1 ☐, 3½" x 3½"
	B: Cut 1 ◺, 3⅞" x 3⅞"
	C: Cut 1 ◺, 6⅞" x 6⅞" (1 left over)

Grandma's Hopscotch

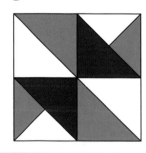 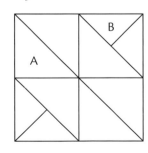 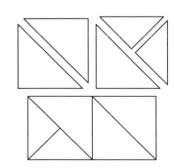

☐ ▦	**A:** Cut 1 ◺, 3⅞" x 3⅞", from *each*	**B:** Cut 1 ⊠, 4¼" x 4¼", from *each* (2 left over of *each* color)
▪	**A:** Cut 1 ◺, 3⅞" x 3⅞"	

Granddad's Plaids

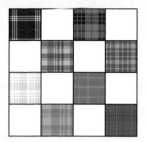 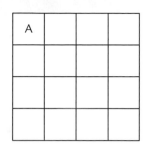 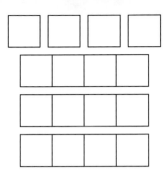

		A: Cut 8 ☐, 2" x 2"
Assorted plaids		A: Cut 8 ☐ *total*, 2" x 2"

Pop-Pop's Bow Tie

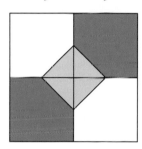 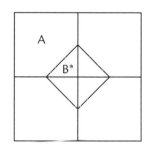 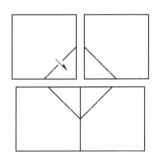

		A: Cut 2 ☐, 3½" x 3½", from *each*
		B: Cut 4 ◨, 2" x 2"✻

Refer to page 117 to place B squares in corners of A squares and sew on the diagonal line to form small triangles.

Thrifty

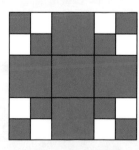 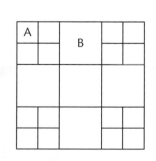 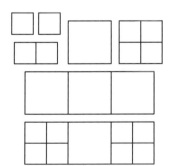

☐	A: Cut 8 ☐, 1½" x 1½"			
▦	A: Cut 8 ☐, 1½" x 1½"		B: Cut 1 ☐, 2½" x 2½"	
▦	B: Cut 4 ☐, 2½" x 2½"			

First Love

Notes from Mimi's Journal

Every once in a while, when I get together with friends from high school, there are certain "boys" we still talk about. First loves are special because they are forever young! I wonder what those "dreamboats" look like now!

Inspiration

- Will your hearts always be woven together?
- Remember your first kiss? Of course!
- Did you dream of "Diamonds" on your fingers?
- Do you remember this time as a "Whirlwind" of emotions?
- Did you ever visit a "Lover's Lane"?

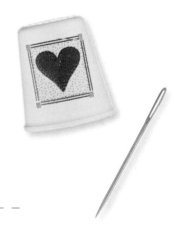

Key to My Diary

I made this block for my Diary quilt because . . .

- -

- -

- -

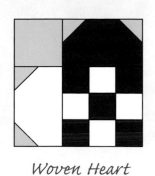

Woven Heart

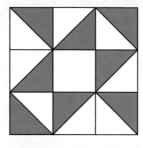

Lover's Lane

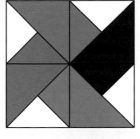

Whirlwind

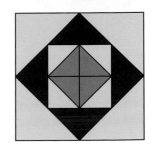

Diamonds

Hearts and Flowers

Diamonds

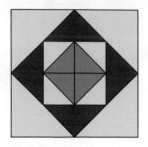 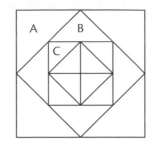 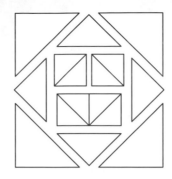

◻ (light)	**A:** Cut 2 ◺, 3⅞" x 3⅞"	**C:** Cut 2 ◺, 2⅜" x 2⅜"	
◼ (dark)	**B:** Cut 1 ⊠, 4¼" x 4¼"		
◼ (medium)	**C:** Cut 2 ◺, 2⅜" x 2⅜"		

Hearts

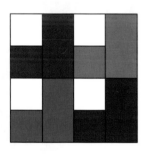 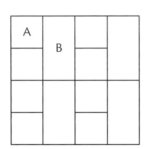 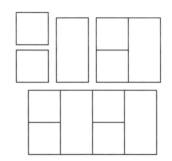

◻	**A:** Cut 4 ◻, 2" x 2"		
4 different reds or pinks	**A:** Cut 1 ◻, 2" x 2", from *each*	**B:** Cut 1 ▭, 2" x 3½", from *each*	

Woven Heart

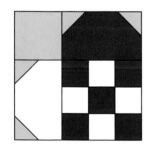 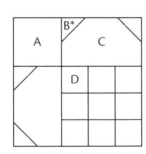 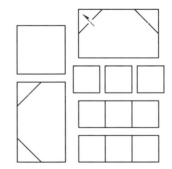

◻ (gray)	**A:** Cut 1 ◻, 2¾" x 2¾"	**B:** Cut 4 ◺, 1⅝" x 1⅝"*	
◼ (black)	**C:** Cut 1 ▭, 2¾" x 4¼"	**D:** Cut 5 ◻, 1¾" x 1¾"	
◻ (white)	**C:** Cut 1 ▭, 2¾" x 4¼"	**D:** Cut 4 ◻, 1¾" x 1¾"	
*Refer to page 117 to place B squares in corners of C rectangles and sew on the diagonal line to form small triangles.			

Lover's Lane

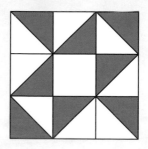 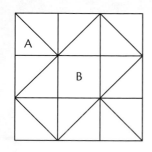 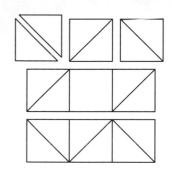

☐	**A:** Cut 4 �ण, 2⅞" x 2⅞"	**B:** Cut 1 ☐, 2½" x 2½"	
◼	**A:** Cut 4 ◳, 2⅞" x 2⅞"		

Whirlwind

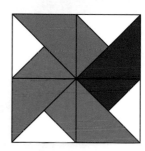 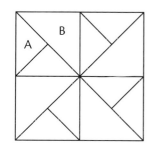 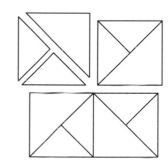

☐	**A:** Cut 1 ⊠, 4¼" x 4¼"	
◼◼◻◼	**A:** Cut 1 ⊠, 4¼" x 4¼", from *each* (3 left over of *each* color)	**B:** Cut 1 ◳, 3⅞" x 3⅞", from *each* (1 left over of *each* color)

Bachelor's Puzzle

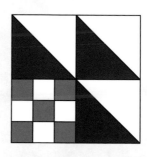 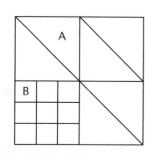 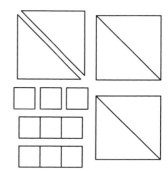

☐	**A:** Cut 2 ◳, 3⅞" x 3⅞" (1 left over)	**B:** Cut 4 ☐, 1½" x 1½"
◼	**A:** Cut 2 ◳, 3⅞" x 3⅞" (1 left over)	
◼	**B:** Cut 5 ☐, 1½" x 1½"	

True Love

Notes from Mimi's Journal

The bridesmaids' dresses in my wedding were pastel "rainbow" colors. I couldn't make a decision on one color. Thank goodness I made the right decision about the groom! I've been married to my true love for 37 years.

Inspiration

- ❧ Remember how exciting it was to plan your wedding?

- ❧ Was your "Trip to the Altar" an adventure?

- ❧ Make a "True Lover's Knot" for your one true love.

- ❧ Add a special button to the top of the "Wedding Ring" to look like your engagement ring.

- ❧ Are you a "Contrary Wife"? Keep it a secret as you stitch this block!

Key to My Diary

I made this block for my Diary quilt because . . .

- -

- -

- -

Double Wedding Ring

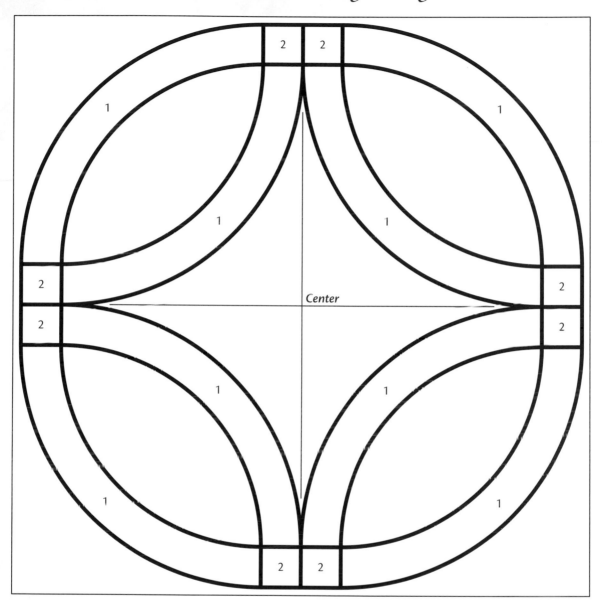

Center

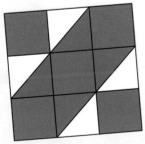

Contrary Wife

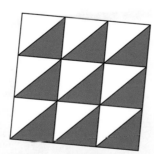

Trip to the Altar

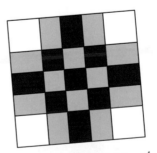

True Lover's Knot

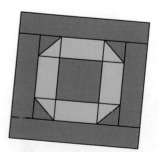

Wedding Ring

Love Knot

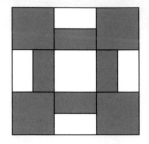

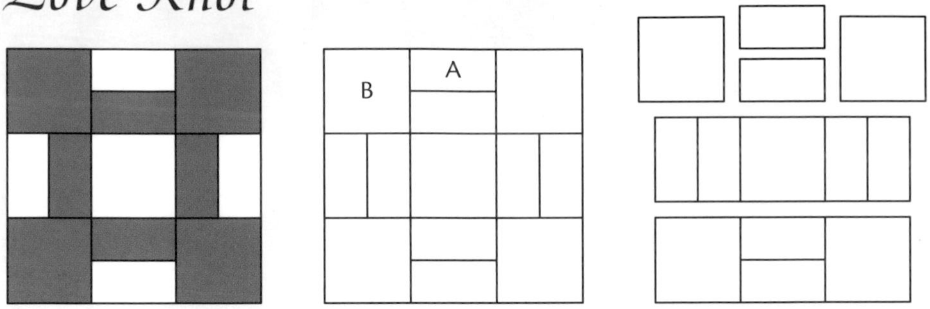

		A: Cut 4 ▭ , 1½" x 2½"	B: Cut 1 ☐ , 2½" x 2½"
		A: Cut 4 ▭ , 1½" x 2½"	B: Cut 4 ☐ , 2½" x 2½"

Steps to the Altar

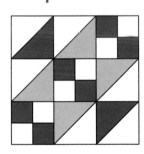
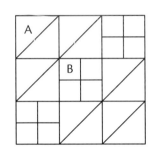
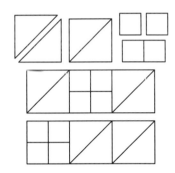

		A: Cut 3 ◿ , 2⅞" x 2⅞"	B: Cut 6 ☐ , 1½" x 1½"
		A: Cut 2 ◺ , 2⅞" x 2⅞"	
		A: Cut 1 ◿ , 2⅞" x 2⅞"	B: Cut 6 ☐ , 1½" x 1½"

Trip to the Altar

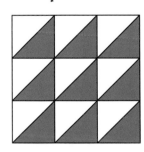
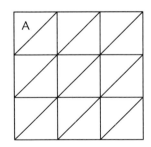
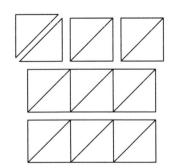

		A: Cut 5 ◿ , 2⅞" x 2⅞", from *each*
		(1 left over of *each* color)

True Lover's Knot

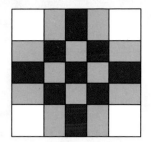 

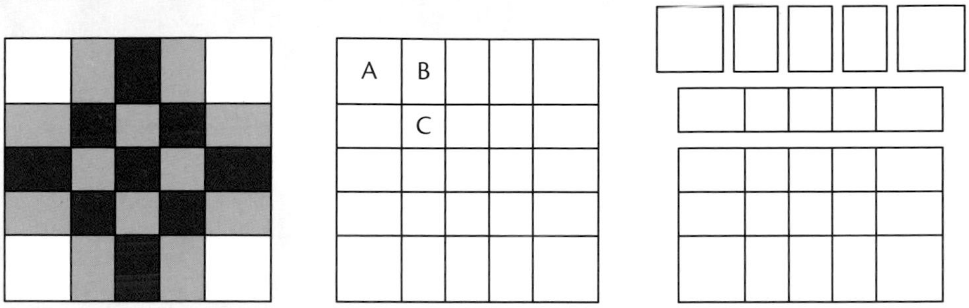

	A: Cut 4 ▢, 2" x 2"		
⬛	B: Cut 4 ▭, 1½" x 2"	C: Cut 5 ▢, 1½" x 1½"
🟩	B: Cut 8 ▭, 1½" x 2"	C: Cut 4 ▢, 1½" x 1½"

Contrary Wife

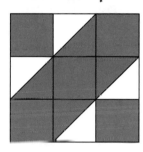 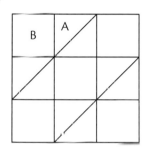 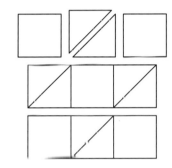

	A: Cut 2 ◩, 2⅞" x 2⅞", from *each*
▢ 🟪	
🟪	B: Cut 5 ▢, 2½" x 2½"

Wedding Ring

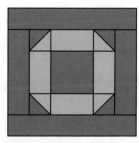 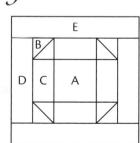 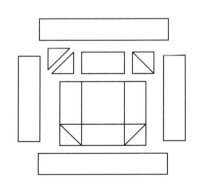

	A: Cut 1 ▢, 2½" x 2½"	B: Cut 2 ◩, 1⅞" x 1⅞"
🟪	D: Cut 2 ▭, 1½" x 4½"	E: Cut 2 ▭, 1½" x 6½"
🟩	B: Cut 2 ◩, 1⅞" x 1⅞"	C: Cut 4 ▭, 1½" x 2½"

Home

Notes from Mimi's Journal

*I've lived in several houses, but there are
two that I consider the "cornerstones" of
my life. I grew up in a Baltimore row
house with close neighborhood friends.
Now I live in our little cottage where
my children grew up. That's home.*

Inspiration

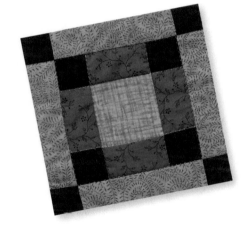

- 🌿 Have you lived in the same house forever?
- 🌿 Did you move when you were growing up?
- 🌿 Have you ever lived in a "Log Cabin"?
- 🌿 Have you purchased or built a "New Home"?
- 🌿 Are you always "Homeward Bound" on holidays?

Key to My Diary

I made this block for my Diary quilt because . . .

- -

- -

- -

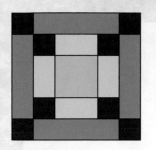

Chimneys and
Cornerstones

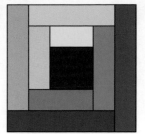

Log Cabin

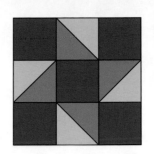

Cottage

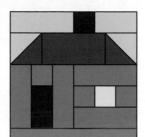

New Home

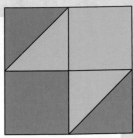

Homeward Bound

House in the Village

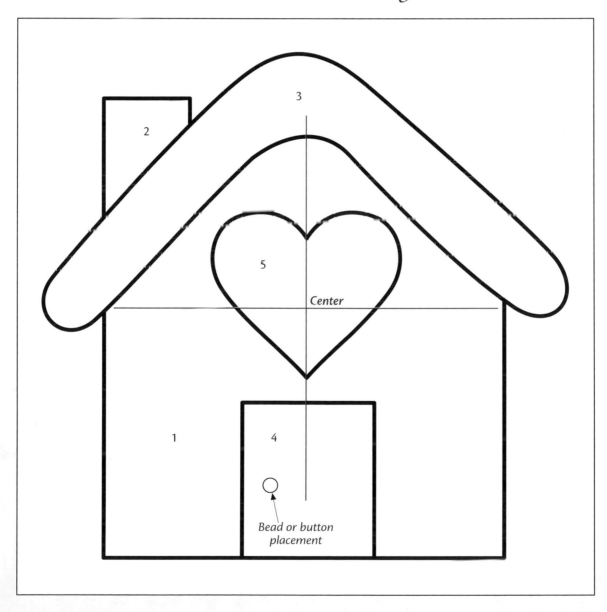

Bead or button
placement

Chimneys and Cornerstones

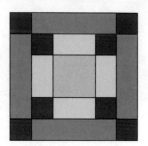 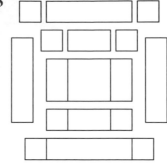

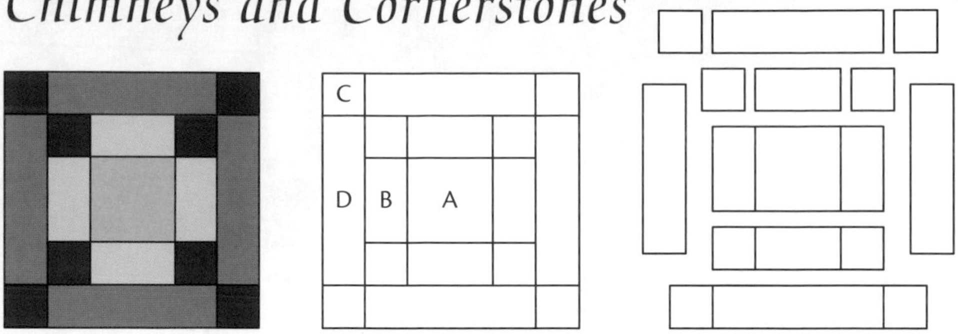

	A: Cut 1 ▢, 2½" x 2½"		**C:** Cut 8 ▢, 1½" x 1½"
	B: Cut 4 ▭, 1½" x 2½"		**D:** Cut 4 ▭, 1½" x 4½"

Homespun

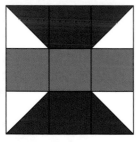 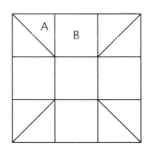 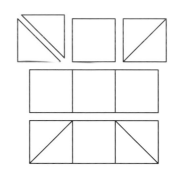

	A: Cut 2 ◺, 2⅞" x 2⅞"		
	A: Cut 2 ◺, 2⅞" x 2⅞"	**B:** Cut 2 ▢, 2½" x 2½"	
	B: Cut 3 ▢, 2½" x 2½"		

Log Cabin

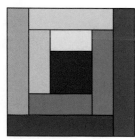 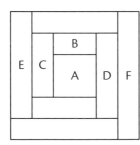 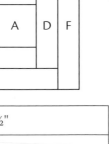 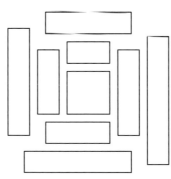

	A: Cut 1 ▢, 2½" x 2½"		**D:** Cut 1 ▭, 1½" x 4½", from *each*
	B: Cut 1 ▭, 1½" x 2½"		**E:** Cut 1 ▭, 1½" x 5½", from *each*
	C: Cut 1 ▭, 1½" x 3½", from *each*		**F:** Cut 1 ▭, 1½" x 6½"

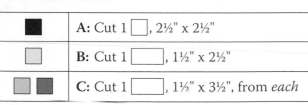

Cottage

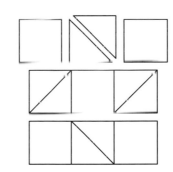

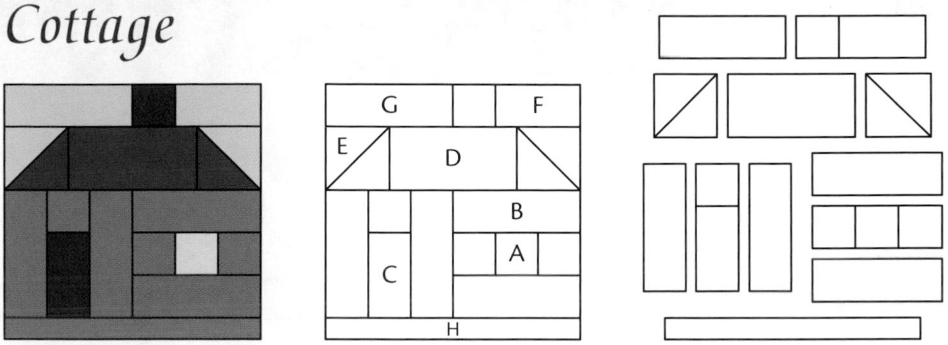

■	**A:** Cut 1 ▢, 1½" x 1½"		
■	**A:** Cut 1 ▢, 1½" x 1½"	**C:** Cut 1 ▭, 1½" x 2½"	
■	**A:** Cut 3 ▢, 1½" x 1½"	**B:** Cut 4 ▭, 1½" x 3½"	
■	**D:** Cut 1 ▭, 2" x 3½"	**E:** Cut 1 ◿, 2⅜" x 2⅜"	
■	**E:** Cut 1 ◿, 2⅜" x 2⅜"	**F:** Cut 1 ▭, 1½" x 2½"	**G:** Cut 1 ▭, 1½" x 3½"
■	**H:** Cut 1 ▭, 1" x 6½"		

New Home

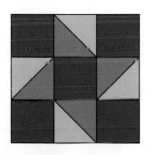

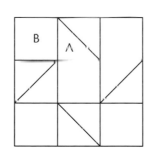

■ ■	**A:** Cut 2 ◿, 2⅞" x 2⅞", from *each*	
■	**B:** Cut 5 ▢, 2½" x 2½"	

Homeward Bound

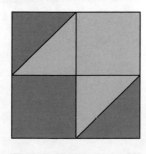

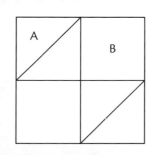

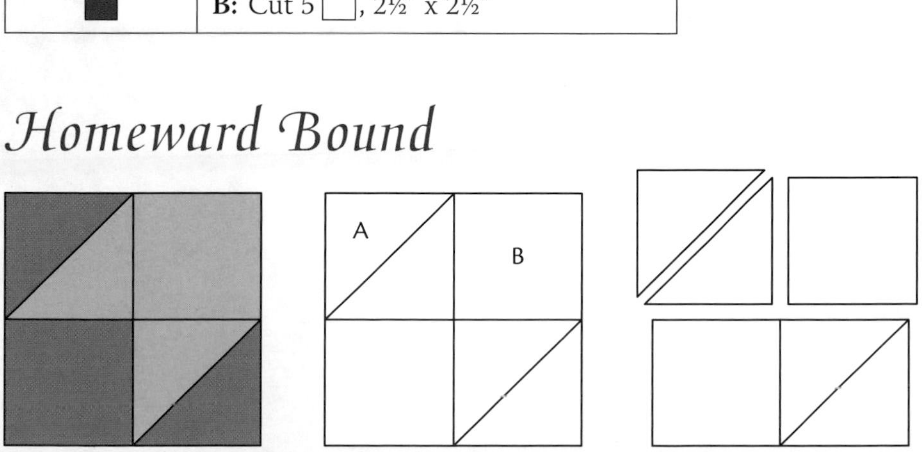

■ ■	**A:** Cut 1 ◿, 3⅞" x 3⅞", from *each*	**B:** Cut 1 ▢, 3½" x 3½", from *each*

Children

Notes from Mimi's Journal

I made my very first quilt before my first son, Jon, was born in 1975. It is an appliquéd quilt with Sunbonnet Sue and Overall Bill. Ryan was born in 1978. His quilt is a blue and gold patchwork star. It was wonderful to wrap my babies in my handmade quilts!

Inspiration

- ❧ The appliqué pattern here is a boy; the girl pattern is on page 19.

- ❧ Don't you just love to hold a new baby wrapped in a quilt?

- ❧ Did your children have favorite toys: "Pinwheels" or "Spinning Tops"?

- ❧ Did you ever feel like a "Hen" with her chicks as you collected your children from school?

- ❧ Did you feel like you released your "Birds in the Air" when your children left home?

Key to My Diary

I made this block for my Diary quilt because . . .

- -

- -

- -

Overall Bill

To make the pocket hanky, cut a 1" square of fabric and fold it in half diagonally, wrong sides together. Fold each side point down to the center point, overlapping the points slightly; baste. Appliqué the pocket, leaving the top unstitched. Insert the hanky into the pocket using tweezers. Appliqué the top edge of the pocket, taking a few stitches all the way through the background to secure the hanky. Leave the top of the hanky unstitched.

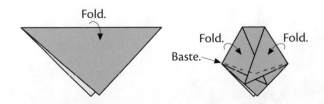

Refer to page 8 to chain stitch the suspenders.

Pinwheels

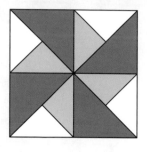 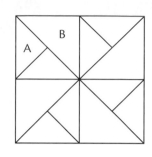 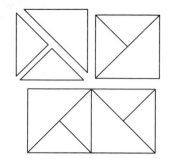

⬜ 🟩	**A:** Cut 1 ⊠, 4¼" x 4¼", from *each*	
🟦	**B:** Cut 2 ◹, 3⅞" x 3⅞"	

Birds in the Air

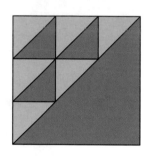 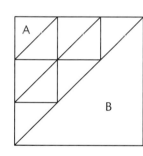 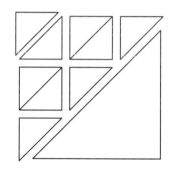

🟩	**A:** Cut 3 ◹, 2⅞" x 2⅞"	
🟦	**A:** Cut 2 ◹, 2⅞" x 2⅞" (1 left over)	**B:** Cut 1 ◹, 6⅞" x 6⅞" (1 left over)

Baby Bunting

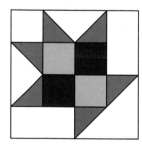 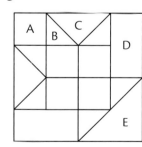 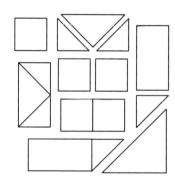

⬜	**A:** Cut 1 ⬜, 2" x 2"	**C:** Cut 1 ⊠, 4¼" x 4¼" (2 left over)	
	D: Cut 2 ▭, 2" x 3½"	**E:** Cut 1 ◹, 3⅞" x 3⅞" (1 left over)	
🟦	**B:** Cut 3 ◹, 2⅜" x 2⅜"		
⬛ 🟪	**A:** Cut 2 ⬜, 2" x 2", from *each*		

Spinning Top

 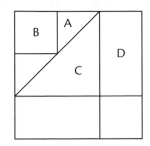 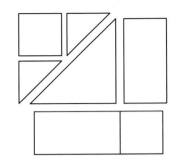

☐	**A:** Cut 1 ◹, 2⅞" x 2⅞"	**D:** Cut 2 ▭, 2½" x 4½"		
◼	**B:** Cut 2 ☐, 2½" x 2½"	**C:** Cut 1 ◹, 4⅞" x 4⅞" (1 left over)		

Hens and Chickens

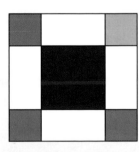 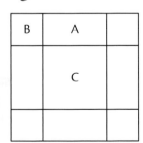 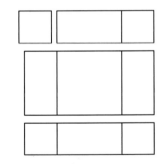

☐ ◼	**A:** Cut 3 ◹, 2⅞" x 2⅞", from *each* (1 left over of *each* color)	
◼	**B:** Cut 1 ☐, 4½" x 4½"	

Children's Delight

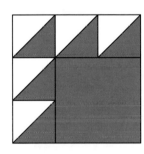 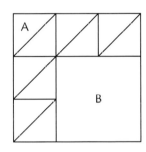 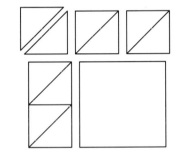

☐	**A:** Cut 4 ▭, 2" x 3½"	
◼ ◼ ◼ ◼	**B:** Cut 1 ☐, 2" x 2", from *each*	
◼	**C:** Cut 1 ☐, 3½" x 3½"	

Pets

Notes from Mimi's Journal

Our family dog had two dark spots over his eyes.
When my son Ryan was eight years old, he brought
home a picture of the dog and begged us to keep him.
I looked at the photo and thought, "What are those
spots that pirates wear over their eyes?" Patches! It was
the perfect "quilted" name for the Dietrich dog.

Inspiration

- Do you have a favorite pet?
- Are you a "dog person" or a "cat person"?
- Are there "Pawprints" on your kitchen floor?
- Use textured fabrics to make the block look like your pet.

Key to My Diary

I made this block for my Diary quilt because . . .

Pawprints

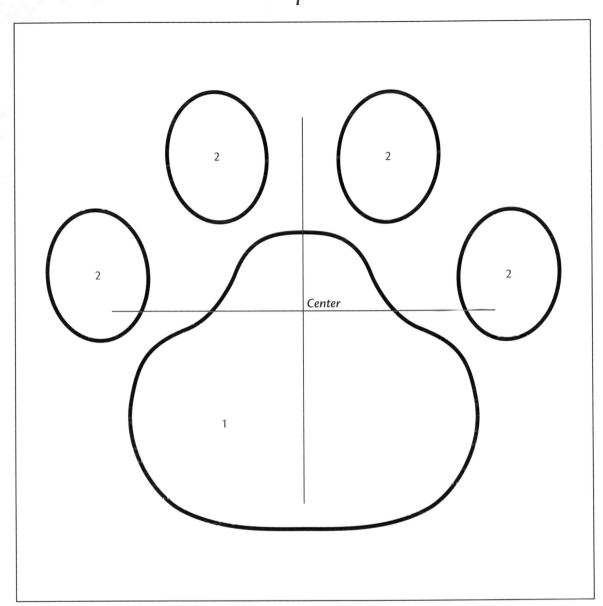

2

2

2

2

Center

1

Puppy's Paws

Dog Bone

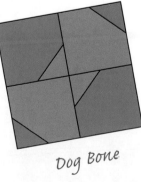

Easy Kitty

Puppy's Paws

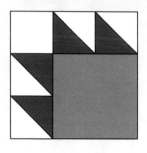 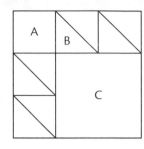 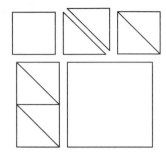

	A: Cut 1 ☐, 2½" x 2½"		■	**B:** Cut 2 ◲, 2⅞" x 2⅞"
	B: Cut 2 ◲, 2⅞" x 2⅞"		▦	**C:** Cut 1 ☐, 4½" x 4½"

Dog Bone

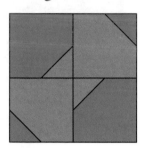 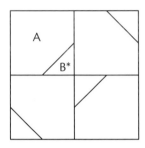 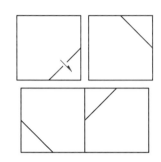

▦ ▦	**A:** Cut 2 ☐, 3½" x 3½", from *each*	**B:** Cut 2 ◳, 2" x 2", from *each**	

**Refer to page 117 to place B squares in corners of A squares
and sew on the diagonal line to form small triangles.*

My Cat

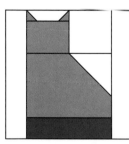 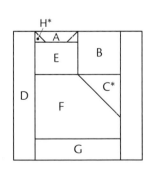 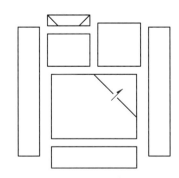

☐	**A:** Cut 1 ▭, 1" x 2½"		**B:** Cut 1 ☐, 2½" x 2½"		
	C: Cut 1 ◳, 2½" x 2½"*		**D:** Cut 2 ▭, 1½" x 6½"		
▦	**E:** Cut 1 ▭, 2" x 2½"		**F:** Cut 1 ▭, 3½" x 4½"	**H:** Cut 2 ◳, 1" x 1"*	
■	**G:** Cut 1 ▭, 1½" x 4½"				

**Refer to page 117 to place H squares in corner of A rectangle and C square in corner
of F rectangle. Sew on the diagonal lines to form triangles.*

Easy Kitty

 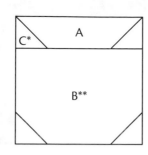 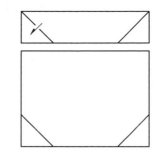

☐	**A:** Cut 1 ▭ , 2" x 6½"		**C:** Cut 2 ◸ , 2" x 2"*	
◼	**B:** Cut 1 ▭ , 5" x 6½"**		**C:** Cut 2 ◸ , 2" x 2"*	

*Refer to page 117 to place C squares in corners of A and B rectangles
and sew on the diagonal line to form triangles.*

**Refer to page 8 to stem stitch the cat's face after the block is completed. You also
can mark the features with a fine-point permanent pen. Add buttons for the eyes.*

Goldfish

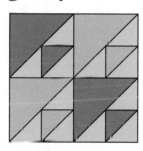 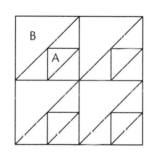 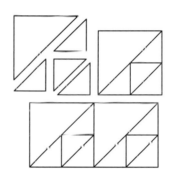

◼	**A:** Cut 6 ◺ , 2⅜" x 2⅜"		
◼ ◼	**A:** Cut 1 ◺ , 2⅜" x 2⅜", from *each*	**B:** Cut 1 ◺ , 3⅜" x 3⅜", from *each*	

Puss in the Corner

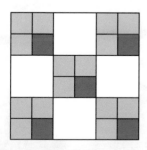 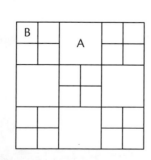 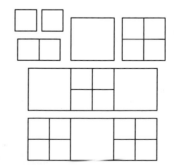

☐	**A:** Cut 4 ☐ , 2½" x 2½"		◼	**B:** Cut 5 ☐ , 1½" x 1½"
◼	**B:** Cut 15 ☐ , 1½" x 1½"			

Patriotism

Notes from Mimi's Journal

For more than 50 years, my hometown has celebrated the Fourth of July with a parade and fireworks. It's fabulous! During the parade, my dad would always stand up and salute every American flag that passed by. That's a fond patriotic memory.

Inspiration

- Celebrate your love for your country! Make these blocks in red, white, and blue.

- Do you have a family member serving in the military?

- Have you ever worked for a political campaign?

- Is the Fourth of July your favorite holiday?

Key to My Diary

I made this block for my Diary quilt because . . .

- -

- -

- -

Stars and Bars

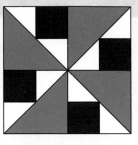

Brave World

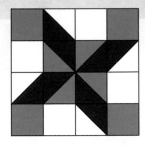

Clay's Choice

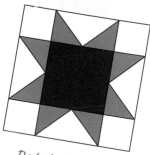

Patriotic Star

Mini Flag

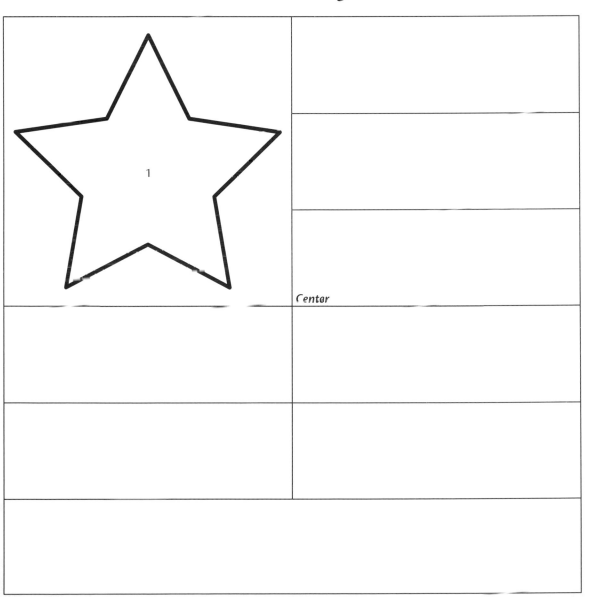

1

Center

Piece the stripe and field sections together first
and then appliqué the star to the field.

Stars and Bars

 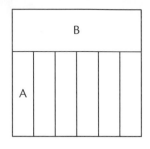 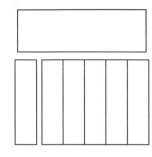

☐ ◼	**A:** Cut 3 ▭ , 1½" x 4½", from *each*	
◼	**B:** Cut 1 ▭ , 2½" x 6½"	

Sew three star buttons to the blue rectangle after the block is completed.

Clay's Choice

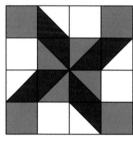 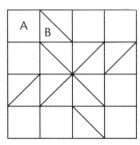 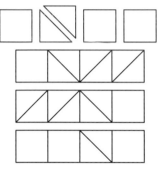

☐ ◼	**A:** Cut 4 ☐ , 2" x 2", from *each*	**B:** Cut 2 ◣ , 2⅜" x 2⅜", from *each*	
◼	**B:** Cut 4 ◣ , 2⅜" x 2⅜"		

Brave World

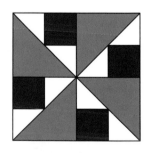 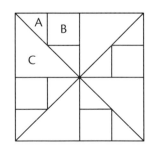 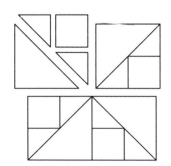

☐	**A:** Cut 4 ◣ , 2⅜" x 2⅜"
◼	**B:** Cut 4 ☐ , 2" x 2"
◼	**C:** Cut 2 ◣ , 3⅞" x 3⅞"

Strength in Union

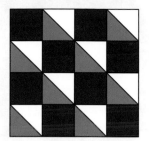 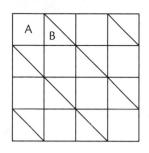

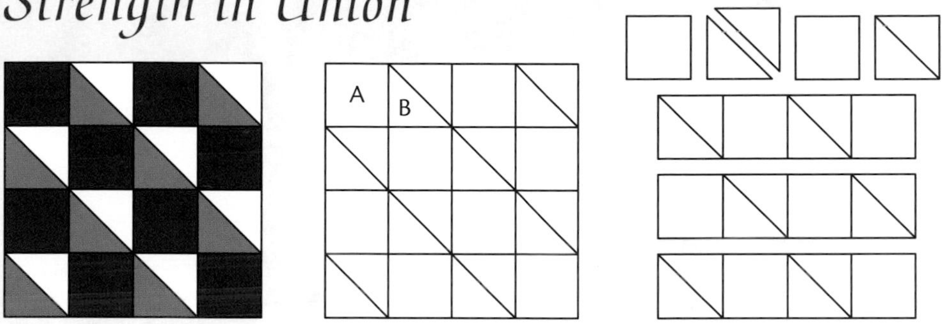

		A: Cut 8 ⬜, 2" x 2"
⬜	🟥	B: Cut 4 ◺, 2⅜" x 2⅜", from *each*

Patriotic Star

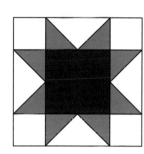 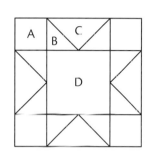 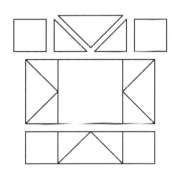

⬜	A: Cut 4 ⬜, 2" x 2"		C: Cut 1 ⊠, 4¼" x 4¼"	
🟥	B: Cut 4 ◺, 2⅜" x 2⅜"			
⬛	D: Cut 1 ⬜, 3½" x 3½"			

State House

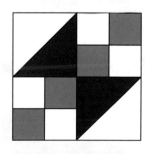 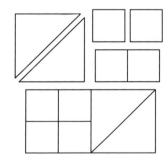

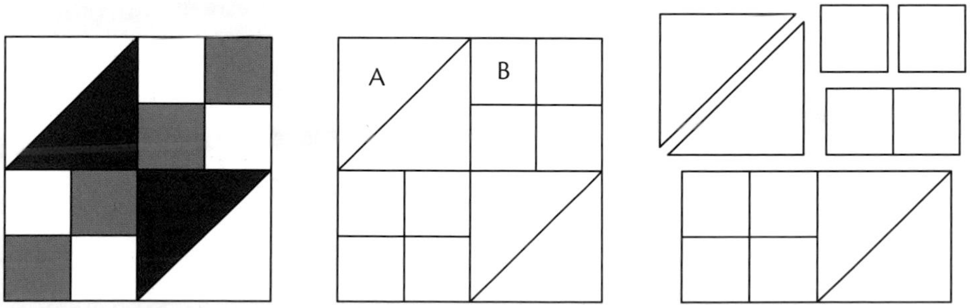

⬜	A: Cut 1 ◿, 3⅞" x 3⅞"	B: Cut 4 ⬜, 2" x 2"	
⬛	A: Cut 1 ◿, 3⅞" x 3⅞"		
🟥	B: Cut 4 ⬜, 2" x 2"		

Religion

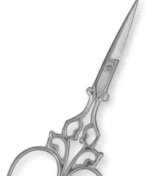

Notes from Mimi's Journal

Faith and hope are a big part of my life. I have faith in God, faith that the world is good, faith that things will go right. I hope that I will be able to handle things if they don't. I have faith in my family and friends, and I hope they have faith in me. This gives me peace.

Inspiration

- Did you grow up in a faith-based family?
- Do you pray for faith, hope, or peace?
- Is quilting a form of meditation for you?
- Do you stitch your faith and hope into quilt blocks?
- Do you take a step on the "Road to Heaven" each day?

Key to My Diary

I made this block for my Diary quilt because . . .

Dove of Peace

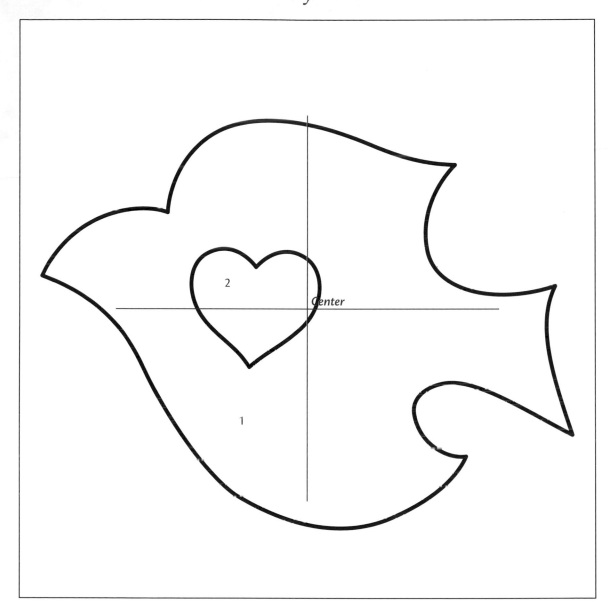

2

Center

1

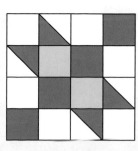

Glory Be

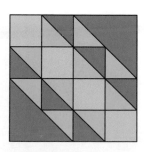

Road to Heaven

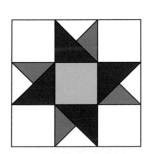

Star of Hope

Star of Hope

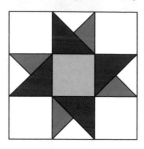 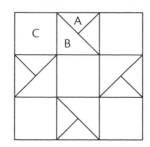 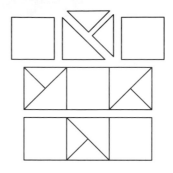

⬜	**A:** Cut 1 ⊠, 3¼" x 3¼"		**C:** Cut 4 ⬜, 2½" x 2½"	
🟦	**C:** Cut 1 ⬜, 2½" x 2½"			
⬛	**B:** Cut 2 ◺, 2⅞" x 2⅞"			
🟫	**A:** Cut 1 ⊠, 3¼" x 3¼"			

Star of David

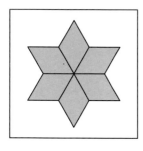 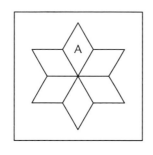 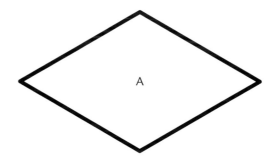

⬜	Cut 1 ⬜, 6½" x 6½"		🟦	Cut 6 using template A

Use the template to cut the shapes from freezer paper. Baste the fabric to the shapes and then hand stitch them together. Appliqué the pieced unit to the center of the background square.

Glory Be

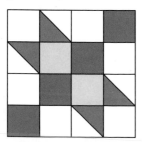 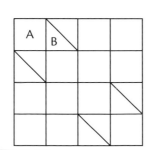 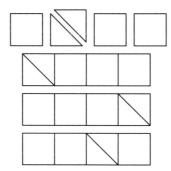

⬜	**A:** Cut 6 ⬜, 2" x 2"		**B:** Cut 2 ◹, 2⅜" x 2⅜"		🟨	**A:** Cut 2 ⬜, 2" x 2"
🟥	**B:** Cut 2 ◺, 2⅜" x 2⅜"				🟫	**A:** Cut 4 ⬜, 2" x 2"

Jacob's Ladder

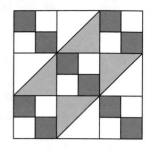 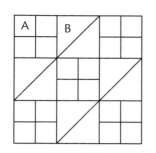 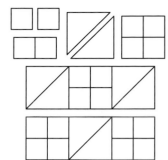

	A: Cut 10 ▢, 1½" x 1½"	B: Cut 2 ◺, 2⅞" x 2⅞"
	A: Cut 10 ▢, 1½" x 1½"	
	B: Cut 2 ◺, 2⅞" x 2⅞"	

Road to Heaven

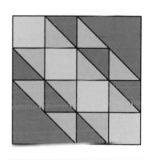 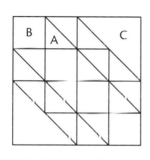 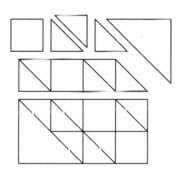

	A: Cut 5 ◺, 2⅜" x 2⅜"	
	A: Cut 3 ◺, 2⅜" x 2⅜"	C: Cut 1 ◺, 3⅞" x 3⅞"
	B: Cut 4 ▢, 2" x 2"	

King's Crown

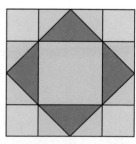 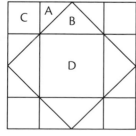 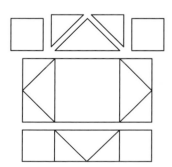

	A: Cut 4 ◺, 2⅜" x 2⅜"	D: Cut 1 ▢, 3½" x 3½"
	B: Cut 1 ⊠, 4¼" x 4¼"	
	C: Cut 4 ▢, 2" x 2"	

Country Life

Notes from Mimi's Journal

My Mom grew up on a farm in rural Mississippi. Her childhood home is still in the family and I love to visit, with its wonderful open space, clean air, a pond, and a very real sense of history. I will always remember Aunt Helen cooking biscuits from scratch, preparing fresh vegetables, and baking sweet potato pie in the country kitchen.

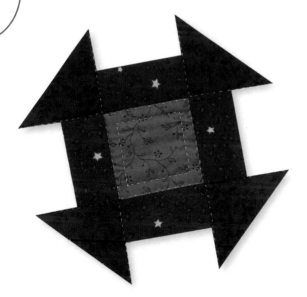

Inspiration

- 🌿 Did you grow up on a farm in the country?
- 🌿 Did you help take care of animals?
- 🌿 Do you have fond memories of visiting a family farm?
- 🌿 Do you love to take walks or go for rides in the country?
- 🌿 Have you ever eaten "Corn and Beans" straight from a country garden?

Key to My Diary

I made this block for my Diary quilt because . . .

Country Bird

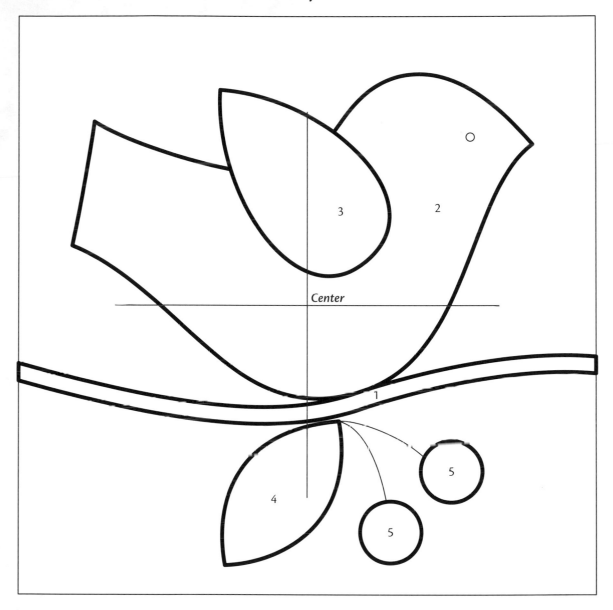

Center

Refer to page 8 to stem stitch the cherry stems
and make a French knot for the bird's eye.

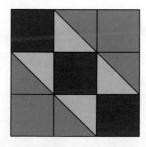

Country Roads

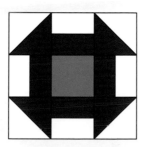

Hole in the
Barn Door

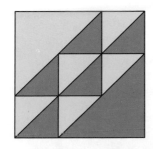

Corn and Beans

Country Roads

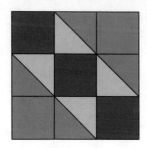 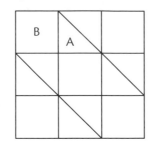 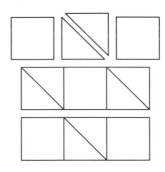

⬜	**A:** Cut 2 ◨, 2⅞" x 2⅞"	
⬜	**A:** Cut 2 ◨, 2⅞" x 2⅞"	**B:** Cut 2 ⬜, 2½" x 2½"
⬛	**B:** Cut 3 ⬜, 2½" x 2½"	

Flock of Geese

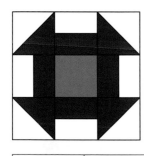  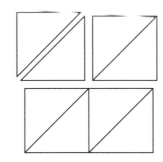

⬛ ⬜	**A:** Cut 2 ◨, 3⅞" x 3⅞", from *each*	

Hole in the Barn Door

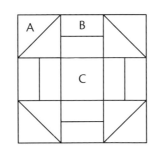 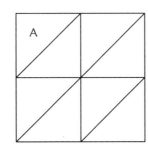 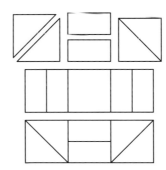

⬜ ⬛	**A:** Cut 2 ◨, 2⅞" x 2⅞", from *each*	**B:** Cut 4 ▭, 1½" x 2½", from *each*
⬛	**C:** Cut 1 ⬜, 2½" x 2½"	

Split Rail Fence

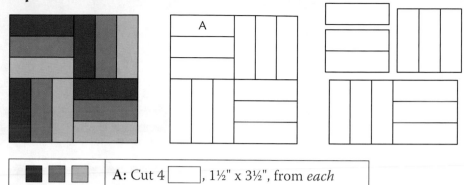

▮ ▮ ▮	**A:** Cut 4 ▭ , 1½" x 3½", from *each*

Corn and Beans

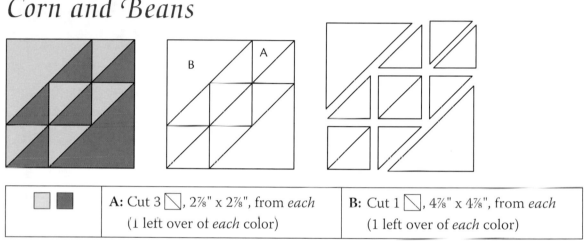

▢ ▮	**A:** Cut 3 ◺, 2⅞" x 2⅞", from *each* (1 left over of *each* color)	**B:** Cut 1 ◺, 4⅞" x 4⅞", from *each* (1 left over of *each* color)

Shoo Fly

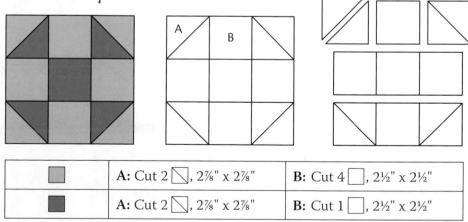

▮	**A:** Cut 2 ◺, 2⅞" x 2⅞"	**B:** Cut 4 ▢, 2½" x 2½"
▮	**A:** Cut 2 ◺, 2⅞" x 2⅞"	**B:** Cut 1 ▢, 2½" x 2½"

Celebrations

Notes from Mimi's Journal

I love to celebrate birthdays, holidays, weddings, graduations, and showers. I'd love to have tea and cupcakes every day! When I was first married, I learned to decorate cakes. It's a great way to celebrate the people in my life and let them know how special they are to me. That's what it's all about!

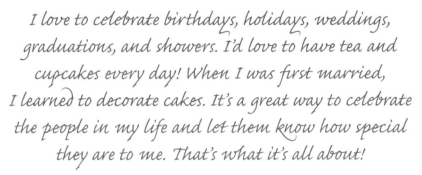

Inspiration

- What's your favorite holiday?
- Do you love family celebrations and traditions?
- Have you ever had an especially memorable birthday celebration?
- Did you ever get special jewelry or a "Jewel Box" for a present?
- Light a candle on the Cupcake block for a special birthday!

Key to My Diary

I made this block for my Diary quilt because . . .

_____

_____

_____

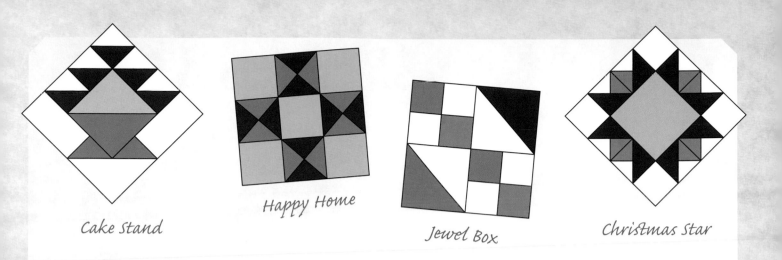

Cake Stand

Happy Home

Jewel Box

Christmas Star

Cupcake

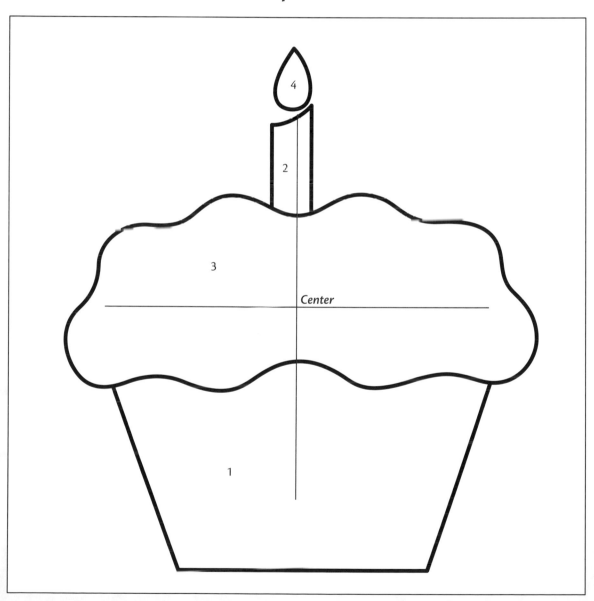

Cake Stand

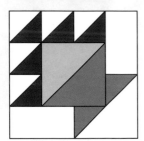 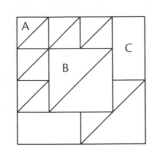 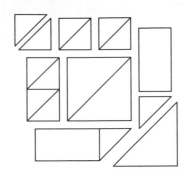

⬜	**A:** Cut 3 ◺, 2⅜" x 2⅜" (1 left over)	**B:** Cut 1 ◺, 3⅞" x 3⅞" (1 left over)	**C:** Cut 2 ▭, 2" x 3½"
🟦	**B:** Cut 1 ◺, 3⅞" x 3⅞" (1 left over)		
🔷	**A:** Cut 1 ◺, 2⅜" x 2⅜"	**B:** Cut 1 ◺, 3⅞" x 3⅞" (1 left over)	
⬛	**A:** Cut 3 ◺, 2⅜" x 2⅜" (1 left over)		

Christmas Star

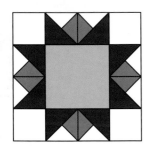 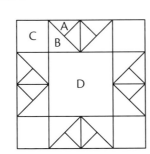 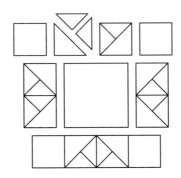

⬜	**A:** Cut 2 ⊠, 2¾" x 2¾"	**C:** Cut 4 ▢, 2" x 2"		🟩	**D:** Cut 1 ▢, 3½" x 3½"
🟥	**A:** Cut 2 ⊠, 2¾" x 2¾"			⬛	**B:** Cut 4 ◺, 2⅜" x 2⅜"

Jewel Box

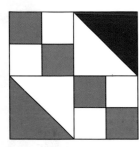 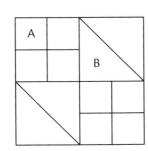 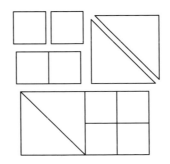

⬜	**A:** Cut 4 ▢, 2" x 2"	**B:** Cut 1 ◺, 3⅞" x 3⅞"
🟪 🟪	**A:** Cut 2 ▢, 2" x 2", from *each*	
⬛ 🟪	**B:** Cut 1 ◺, 3⅞" x 3⅞", from *each* (1 left over of *each* color)	

Party Favor

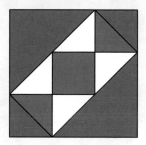 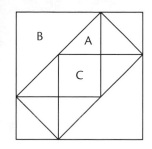 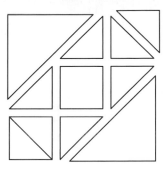

⬜	**A:** Cut 2 ◨, 2⅞" x 2⅞"		
🟫	**A:** Cut 1 ◨, 2⅞" x 2⅞"	**C:** Cut 1 ⬜, 2½" x 2½"	
🟪	**A:** Cut 1 ◨, 2⅞" x 2⅞"	**B:** Cut 1 ◨, 4⅞" x 4⅞"	

Happy Home

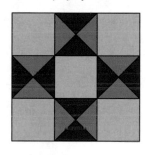 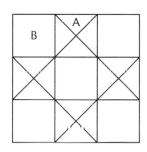 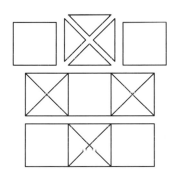

⬛ 🟫	**A:** Cut 2 ⊠, 3¼" x 3¼", from *each*
🟩	**B:** Cut 5 ⬜, 2½" x 2½"

Present

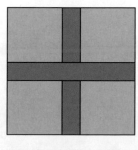 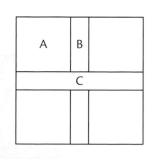 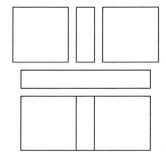

🟩	**A:** Cut 4 ⬜, 3" x 3"		
🟥	**B:** Cut 2 ▭, 1½" x 3"	**C:** Cut 1 ▭, 1½" x 6½"	

Tie a 1"-wide length of ribbon in a bow and sew it to the center of C.

Friends

Notes from Mimi's Journal

Mom always told me to treasure my friends—and I do. I have friends that I have known for more than 50 years! I can remember a song we sang when we were Girl Scouts. "Make new friends but keep the old. One is silver and the other is gold." How true. I love you all!

Inspiration

- 🌿 Who is your best friend? What are her favorite colors?
- 🌿 What's the nicest thing a friend has ever done for you?
- 🌿 What's the best thing you have ever done for a friend?
- 🌿 You have to make a block for your friends!

Key to My Diary

I made this block for my Diary quilt because . . .

--- --- --- --- --- --- --- --- --- --- --- ---

--- --- --- --- --- --- --- --- --- --- --- ---

--- --- --- --- --- --- --- --- --- --- --- ---

Heart and Hand

1

Center

2

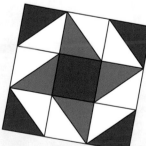

Friendship Star

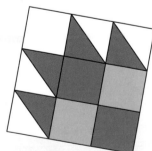

Best Friend

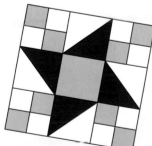

Friendly Hand

Friendship Star

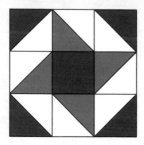 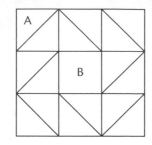 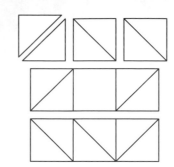

⬜	**A:** Cut 4 ◺, 2⅞" x 2⅞"		
🟥	**A:** Cut 2 ◺, 2⅞" x 2⅞"		
🟥	**A:** Cut 2 ◺, 2⅞" x 2⅞"	**B:** Cut 1 ⬜, 2½" x 2½"	

Best Friend

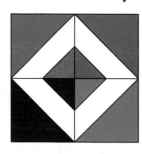 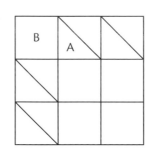 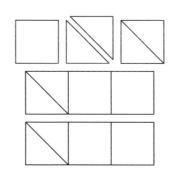

⬜	**A:** Cut 2 ◺, 2⅞" x 2⅞"	**B:** Cut 1 ⬜, 2½" x 2½"
🟥	**A:** Cut 2 ◺, 2⅞" x 2⅞"	
🟥 🟧	**B:** Cut 2 ⬜, 2½" x 2½", from *each*	

Friendship

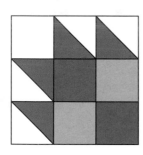 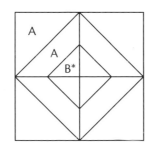 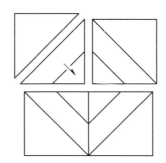

⬜	**A:** Cut 2 ◺, 3⅞" x 3⅞"		
🟥🟥🟥🟥	**A:** Cut 1 ◺, 3⅞" x 3⅞", from *each* (1 left over of *each* color)	**B:** Cut 1 ◻, 2" x 2", from *each**

*Refer to page 117 to place B squares in corners of white A triangles and sew on the diagonal line to form small triangles.

Hand of Friendship

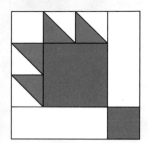 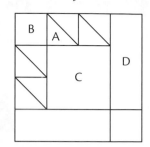 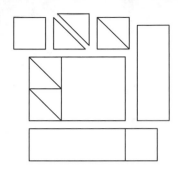

		A: Cut 2 ◺, 2⅜" x 2⅜"	B: Cut 1 ☐, 2" x 2"	D: Cut 2 ▭, 2" x 5"
		A: Cut 2 ◹, 2⅜" x 2⅜"		
		B: Cut 1 ☐, 2" x 2"	C: Cut 1 ☐, 3½" x 3½"	

Next-Door Neighbor

 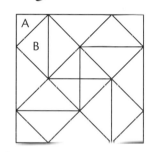 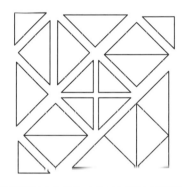

		A: Cut 2 ◺, 2⅜" x 2⅜"	B: Cut 1 ⊠, 4¼" x 4¼"
▪ ▪		A: Cut 1 ◺, 2⅜" x 2⅜", from *each* (1 left over of *each* color)	B: Cut 1 ⊠, 4¼" x 4¼", from *each*

Friendly Hand

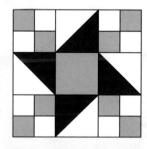 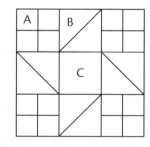 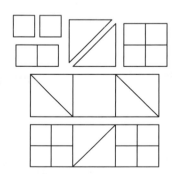

		A: Cut 8 ☐, 1½" x 1½"	B: Cut 2 ◺, 2⅞" x 2⅞"
		A: Cut 8 ☐, 1½" x 1½"	C: Cut 1 ☐, 2½" x 2½"
		B: Cut 2 ◺, 2⅞" x 2⅞"	

Careers

Notes from Mimi's Journal

*Teacher, Mother, Quilter, Writer, Designer . . .
I've had many careers. When people ask me what
I do, my favorite answer is "Quilter" because it
starts a memorable conversation about the quilters
in our lives. I feel creative when I'm surrounded
with fabric, ribbons, buttons, and thread.*

Inspiration

- 🍂 Are you a teacher? You deserve an "Apple"!
- 🍂 Were you inspired by a favorite teacher?
- 🍂 Do you work in the health-care field?
- 🍂 Do you work with law or justice?
- 🍂 Have you climbed the "Ladder of Success"?

Key to My Diary

I made this block for my Diary quilt because . . .

_____

_____

_____

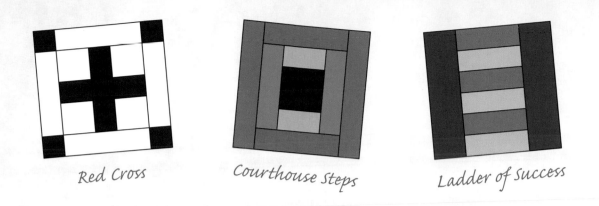

Red Cross   Courthouse Steps   Ladder of Success

Apple for the Teacher

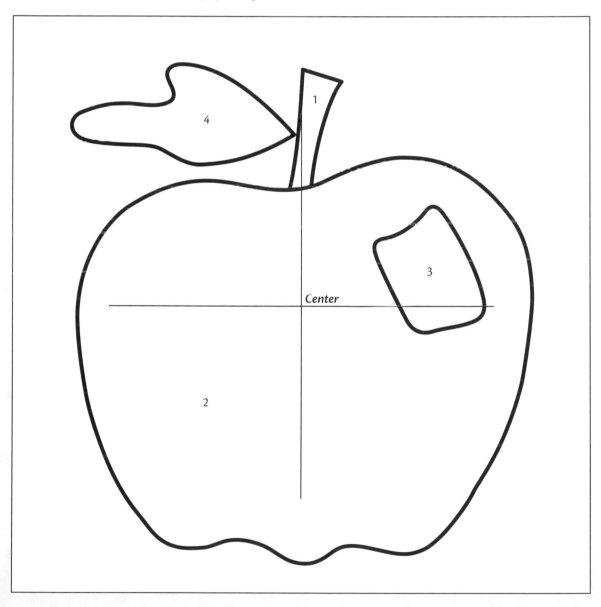

Red Cross

 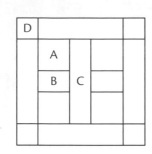 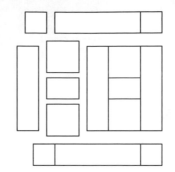

(white)	**A:** Cut 4 ☐, 2" x 2"		**C:** Cut 4 ▭, 1½" x 4½"		
(red)	**B:** Cut 2 ▭, 1½" x 2"		**C:** Cut 1 ▭, 1½" x 4½"	**D:** Cut 4 ☐, 1½" x 1½"	

Monkey Wrench

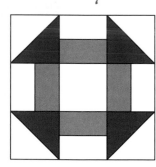 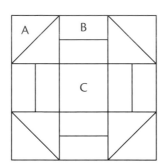 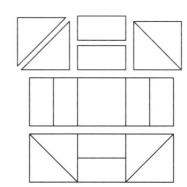

(white)	**A:** Cut 2 ◸, 2⅞" x 2⅞"	**B:** Cut 4 ▭, 1½" x 2½"	**C:** Cut 1 ☐, 2½" x 2½"
(dark)	**A:** Cut 2 ◺, 2⅞" x 2⅞"		
(gray)	**B:** Cut 4 ▭, 1½" x 2½"		

Barrister's Block

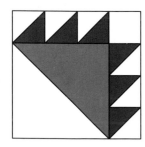 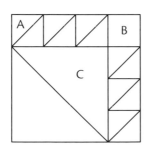 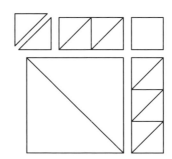

(white)	**A:** Cut 3 ◸, 2⅜" x 2⅜"	**B:** Cut 1 ☐, 2" x 2"	**C:** Cut 1 ◿, 5⅜" x 5⅜" (1 left over)
(dark)	**A:** Cut 3 ◺, 2⅜" x 2⅜"		
(gray)	**C:** Cut 1 ◺, 5⅜" x 5⅜" (1 left over)		

Ladder of Success

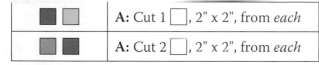	**A:** Cut 3 ▭, 1½" x 3½", from *each*	
	B: Cut 2 ▭, 2" x 6½"	

Building Blocks

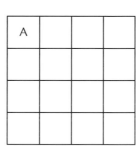

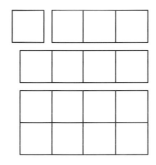

A: Cut 1 ▢, 2" x 2", from *each*	**A:** Cut 3 ▢, 2" x 2", from *each*
A: Cut 2 ▢, 2" x 2", from *each*	**A:** Cut 4 ▢, 2" x 2"

Courthouse Steps

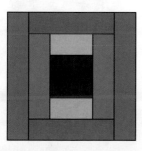

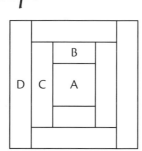

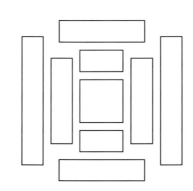

A: Cut 1 ▢, 2½" x 2½"	
B: Cut 2 ▭, 1½" x 2½"	
C: Cut 2 ▭, 1½" x 4½", from *each*	
D: Cut 2 ▭, 1½" x 6½"	

Seasons

Notes from Mimi's Journal

I live in Maryland where we enjoy all of the seasons throughout the year. I love spring and fall when the world changes and the colors are so beautiful. I stitched the Holly block for my quilt because Christmas and my birthday are during the winter. I also love the snow during winter, when it's cozy and warm in my sewing room!

Inspiration

- ❧ What's your favorite season?
- ❧ Do you love the colors of the "Flower Buds" in spring?
- ❧ Do the "Summer Winds" and sunshine feed your soul?
- ❧ Do you love the colors of the "Fall Leaves"?
- ❧ Do "Holly" leaves and "Snowballs" make you think of winter?

Key to My Diary

I made this block for my Diary quilt because . . .

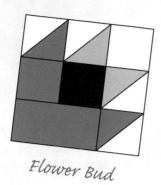

Flower Bud

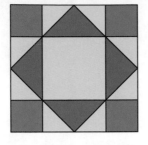

Summer Winds

Fall Leaves

Holly

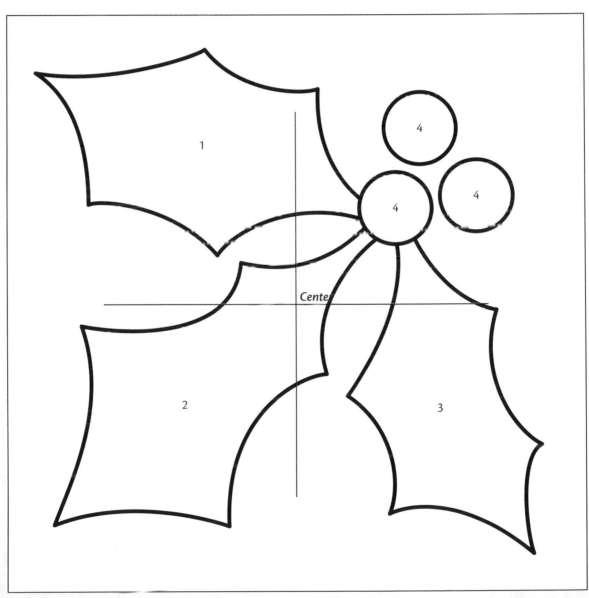

Snowball

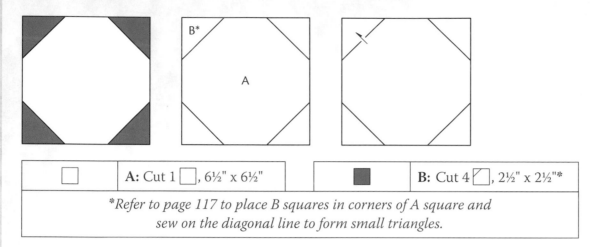

□	**A:** Cut 1 □, 6½" x 6½"		■	**B:** Cut 4 ◹, 2½" x 2½"*	

*Refer to page 117 to place B squares in corners of A square and
sew on the diagonal line to form small triangles.*

Fall Leaves

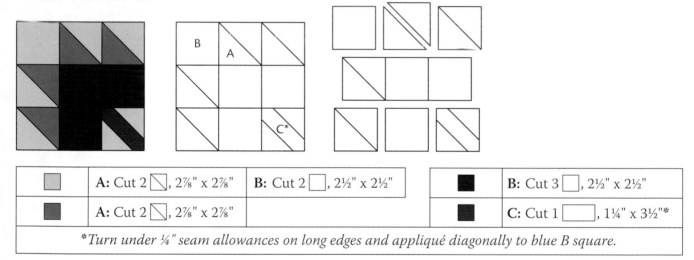

▨	**A:** Cut 2 ◺, 2⅞" x 2⅞"	**B:** Cut 2 □, 2½" x 2½"		■	**B:** Cut 3 □, 2½" x 2½"	
▨	**A:** Cut 2 ◺, 2⅞" x 2⅞"			■	**C:** Cut 1 ▭, 1¼" x 3½"*	

Turn under ¼" seam allowances on long edges and appliqué diagonally to blue B square.

May Basket

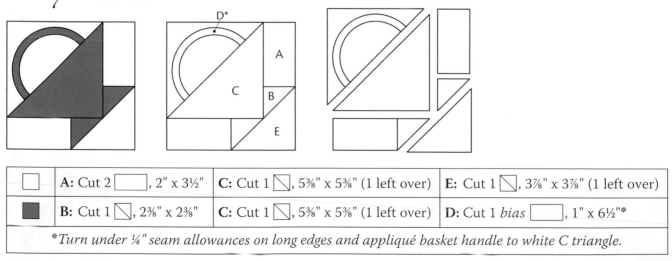

□	**A:** Cut 2 ▭, 2" x 3½"	**C:** Cut 1 ◺, 5⅜" x 5⅜" (1 left over)	**E:** Cut 1 ◺, 3⅞" x 3⅞" (1 left over)		
■	**B:** Cut 1 ◺, 2⅜" x 2⅜"	**C:** Cut 1 ◺, 5⅜" x 5⅜" (1 left over)	**D:** Cut 1 *bias* ▭, 1" x 6½"*		

Turn under ¼" seam allowances on long edges and appliqué basket handle to white C triangle.

Flower Bud

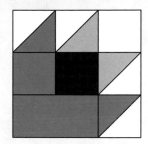 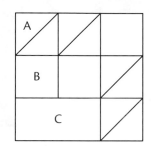 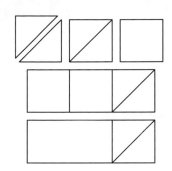

		A	B
	⬜	**A:** Cut 2 ◧, 2⅞" x 2⅞"	**B:** Cut 1 ⬜, 2½" x 2½"
	⬜	**A:** Cut 1 ◩, 2⅞" x 2⅞"	
	⬛	**B:** Cut 1 ⬜, 2½" x 2½"	
	⬜	**A:** Cut 1 ◩, 2⅞" x 2⅞"	**B:** Cut 1 ⬜, 2½" x 2½"	**C:** Cut 1 ▭, 2½" x 4½"

Bluebird

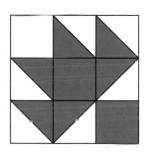 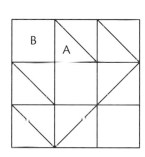 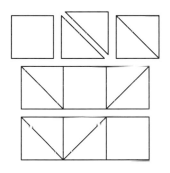

		A	B
	⬜	**A:** Cut 3 ◧, 2⅞" x 2⅞"	**B:** Cut 1 ⬜, 2½" x 2½"
	⬛	**A:** Cut 3 ◧, 2⅞" x 2⅞"	**B:** Cut 2 ⬜, 2½" x 2½"

Summer Winds

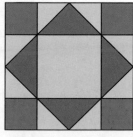 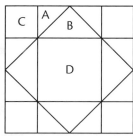 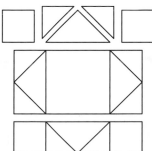

		A	D
	⬜	**A:** Cut 4 ◧, 2⅜" x 2⅜"	**D:** Cut 1 ⬜, 3½" x 3½"
	⬛	**B:** Cut 1 ⊠, 4¼" x 4¼"	
	⬛	**C:** Cut 4 ⬜, 2" x 2"	

Quilting

Notes from Mimi's Journal

I learned to sew when I was 12 years old. Quilting is great because there are so many techniques and fun ways to be creative. My favorite room in my house is my studio. It's full of fabric, buttons, ribbons, and threads, and even when it's messy—especially when it's messy—it's wonderful!

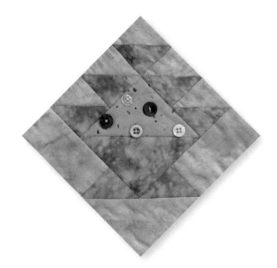

Inspiration

- ❧ What was the first quilt block you made?
- ❧ Do you collect antique buttons? Sew some into the Button Basket or Button Jar blocks.
- ❧ Do you love the feel of old wooden spools?
- ❧ Is your stash a "Calico Puzzle" with all of your favorite pieces?
- ❧ Do you enjoy looking at all the colors in your fabric and thread collection?

Key to My Diary

I made this block for my Diary quilt because . . .

- -

- -

- -

Pincushion

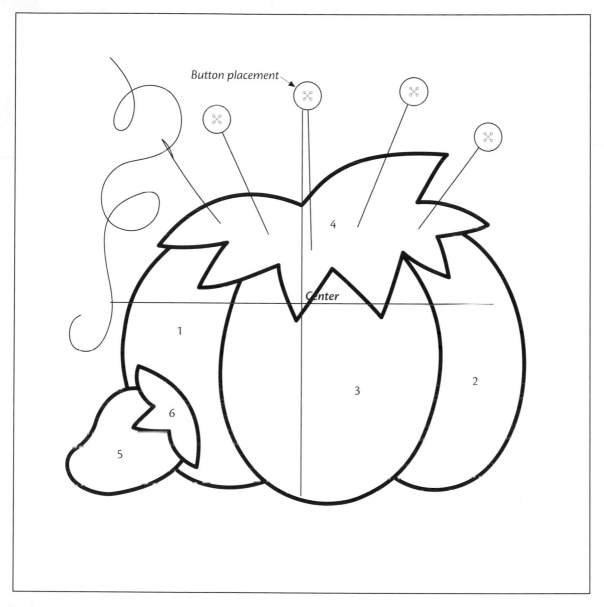

Button placement

Center

1

2

3

4

5

6

Stem stitch the needle, thread, and pin shafts. Add French knots to the strawberry
for seeds. Sew small buttons to the top of the pin shafts for the heads.

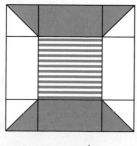

Spool

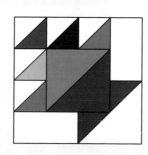

Button Basket

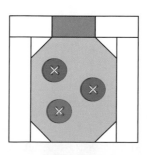

Button Jar

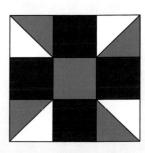

Calico Puzzle

Spool and Bobbin

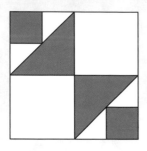 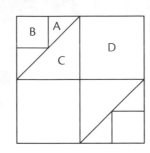 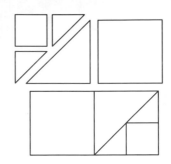

⬜	**A:** Cut 2 ◹, 2⅜" x 2⅜"	**D:** Cut 2 ⬜, 3½" x 3½"
🟦	**B:** Cut 2 ⬜, 2" x 2"	**C:** Cut 1 ◹, 3⅞" x 3⅞"

Button Jar

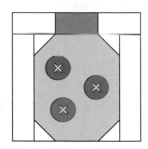 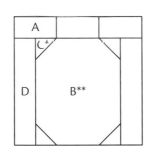 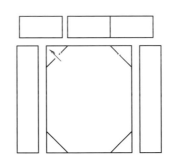

⬜	**A:** Cut 2 ▭, 1½" x 2½"	**C:** Cut 4 ◹, 1½" x 1½"*	**D:** Cut 2 ▭, 1½" x 5½"
🟦	**A:** Cut 1 ▭, 1½" x 2½"		
🟨	**B:** Cut 1 ▭, 4½" x 5½"**		

*Refer to page 117 to place C squares in corners of B rectangle and sew on diagonal line to form small triangles.

**Sew buttons to B rectangle after block is completed.

Spool

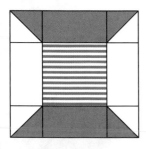 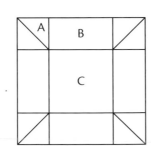 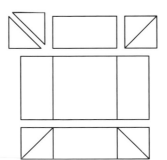

⬜ 🟦	**A:** Cut 2 ◹, 2⅜" x 2⅜", from *each*	**B:** Cut 2 ▭, 2" x 3½", from *each*
▤	**C:** Cut 1 ⬜, 3½" x 3½"	

Button Basket

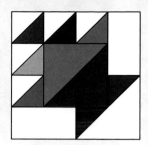 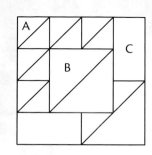 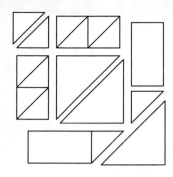

☐	**A:** Cut 3 ◺, 2⅜" x 2⅜" (1 left over)		**B:** Cut 1 ◺, 3⅞" x 3⅞" (1 left over)		**C:** Cut 2 ▭, 2" x 3½"	
■	**A:** Cut 1 ◺, 2⅜" x 2⅜"		**B:** Cut 1 ◺, 3⅞" x 3⅞" (1 left over)			
■	**B:** Cut 1 ◺, 3⅞" x 3⅞" (1 left over)					
■ ■ ■ ■ ■	**A:** Cut 1 ◺, 2⅜" x 2⅜" from *each* (1 left over of *each* color)					

Calico Puzzle

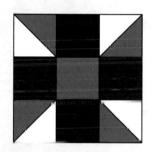 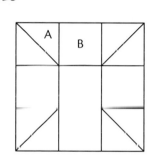 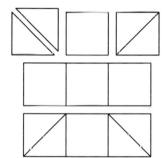

☐	**A:** Cut 2 ◺, 2⅞" x 2⅞"		
■	**A:** Cut 2 ◺, 2⅞" x 2⅞"	**B:** Cut 1 ☐, 2½" x 2½"	
■	**B:** Cut 4 ☐, 2½" x 2½"		

My First Quilt Block

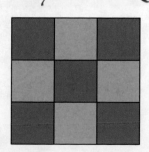 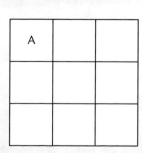 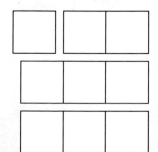

■	**A:** Cut 4 ☐, 2½" x 2½"		■	**A:** Cut 5 ☐, 2½" x 2½"

Travel

Notes from Mimi's Journal

Life is a journey! Quilting has taken me to fabulous places all over the United States. My appliqué needle has been my ticket to adventures in Alaska and Hawaii, California and Cape Cod, Florida and Iowa, and of course, Quilt Festival in Houston, Texas. It's wonderful to travel, but . . . there's no place like home!

Inspiration

- Do you love to travel?
- What's your favorite place you've ever visited?
- Do you love the cool crisp air in the mountains?
- Does your soul long for the peaceful sound of the "Ocean Waves"?
- Would you love to take a "Trip around the World"?

Key to My Diary

I made this block for my Diary quilt because . . .

_____

_____

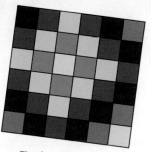

Trip around
the World

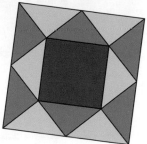

Ocean Waves

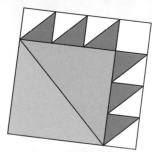

DeleCtable
Mountains

Compass

Trip around the World

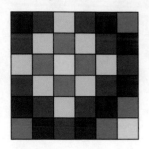 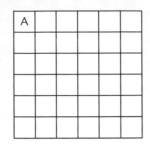

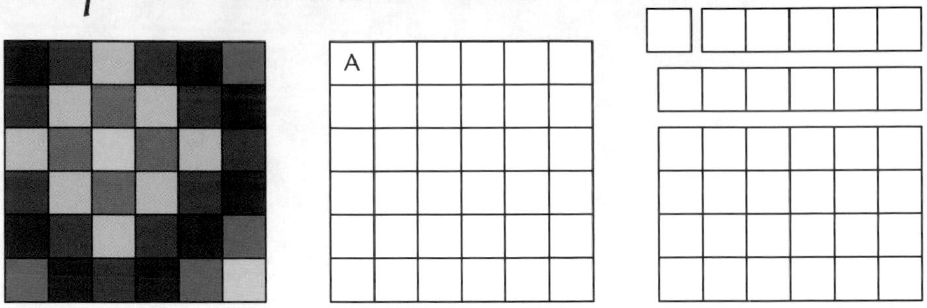

⬜	**A:** Cut 2 ⬜, 1½" x 1½"	
🟪 🟫	**A:** Cut 4 ⬜, 1½" x 1½", from *each*	

⬛ 🟩	**A:** Cut 8 ⬜, 1½" x 1½", from *each*	
⬛	**A:** Cut 10 ⬜, 1½" x 1½"	

Hither and Yon

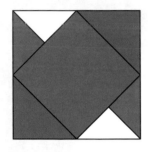 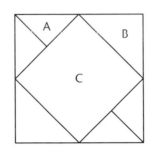 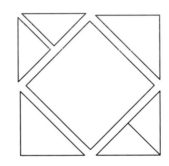

⬜ 🟦	**A:** Cut 1 ⊠, 4¼" x 4¼", from *each* (2 left over of *each* color)	
🟦	**B:** Cut 1 ◥, 3⅞" x 3⅞"	
🟦	**C:** Cut 1 ⬜, 4¾" x 4¾"	

Road to California

 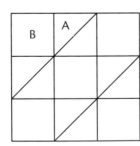 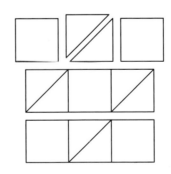

🟨	**A:** Cut 2 ◥, 2⅞" x 2⅞"	**B:** Cut 1 ⬜, 2½" x 2½"
⬛	**A:** Cut 2 ◥, 2⅞" x 2⅞"	
🟥	**A:** Cut 4 ⬜, 2½" x 2½"	

Ocean Waves

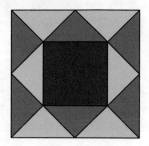 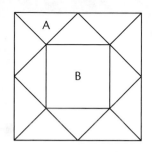 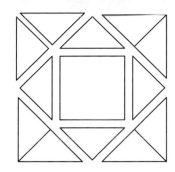

	A: Cut 2 ⊠, 4¼" x 4¼", from *each* (2 left over of *each* color)
	B: Cut 1 ☐, 3½" x 3½"

Delectable Mountains

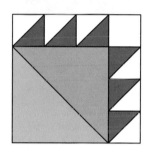 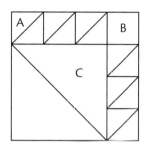 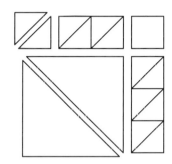

	A: Cut 3 ◺, 2⅜" x 2⅜"		B: Cut 1 ☐, 2" x 2"
	A: Cut 3 ◺, 2⅜" x 2⅜"		
	C: Cut 1 ◺, 5⅜" x 5⅜", from *each* (1 left over of *each* color)		

Northern Lights

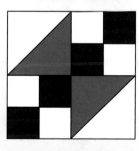 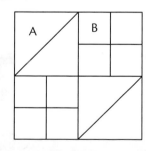 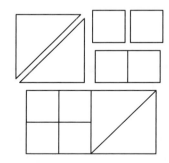

	A: Cut 1 ◹, 3⅞" x 3⅞"		B: Cut 4 ☐, 2" x 2"
	A: Cut 1 ◹, 3⅞" x 3⅞"		
	B: Cut 4 ☐, 2" x 2"		

Hobbies

Notes from Mimi's Journal

My mom played canasta with a group of her best friends for many years. I have played bridge with some of my best friends for more than 30 years. I have become my mother! I just had to include the Card Trick block in my Diary quilt!

Inspiration

- Do you listen to music while you quilt?
- Do you collect "Books," just love to read, or listen to books on tape?
- Do you play checkers or chess?
- If quilting is your hobby, include your favorite block!
- Do you share a hobby with a "Circle of Friends"?

Key to My Diary

I made this block for my Diary quilt because . . .

- -

- -

- -

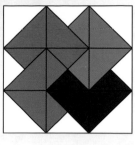

Card Trick

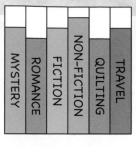

Books

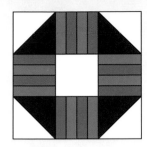

Circle of Friends

Music

Center

Refer to page 8 to embroider lines with an outline stitch and music symbols with a chain stitch. You can also mark the design with a fine-point permanent pen—or crayons!

Card Trick

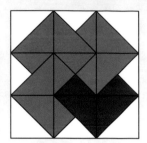 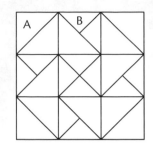 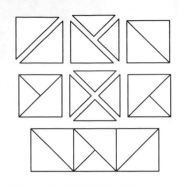

☐	**A:** Cut 2 ◺, 2⅞" x 2⅞"	**B:** Cut 1 ⊠, 3¼" x 3¼"	
■ ■ ■ ■	**A:** Cut 1 ◺, 2⅞" x 2⅞", from *each*	**B:** Cut 1 ⊠, 3¼" x 3¼", from *each* (2 left over of *each* color)	

Books

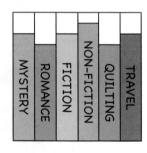 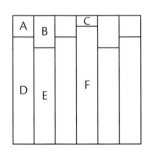 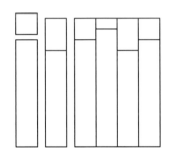

☐	**A:** Cut 3 ☐, 1½" x 1½"	**B:** Cut 2 ▭, 1½" x 2"	**C:** Cut 1 ▭, 1" x 1½"	
■ ■ ■	**D:** Cut 1 ▭, 1½" x 5½", from *each*			
■ ■	**E:** Cut 1 ▭, 1½" x 5", from *each*	*Refer to page 8 to stem stitch desired book titles on D, E, and F rectangles. You can also mark the titles with a fine-point permanent pen.*		
■	**F:** Cut 1 ▭, 1½" x 6"			

Checkerboard

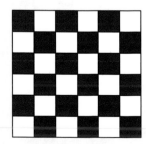 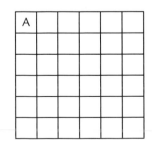 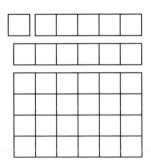

■ ☐	**A:** Cut 18 ☐, 1½" x 1½", from *each*	

Gardening

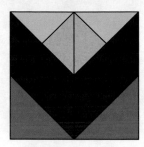 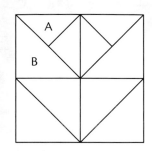 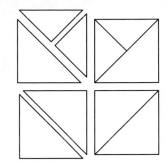

▦ ▦	**A:** Cut 1 ⊠, 4¼" x 4¼", from *each* (2 left over of *each* color)
■	**B:** Cut 2 ◺, 3⅞" x 3⅞"
■	**B:** Cut 1 ◺, 3⅞" x 3⅞"

Square Dance

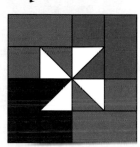 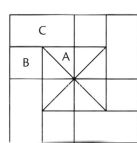 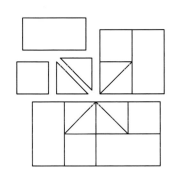

▢	**A:** Cut 2 ◺, 2⅜" x 2⅜"		
■■■■	**A:** Cut 1 ◺, 2⅜" x 2⅜", from *each* (1 left over of *each* color)	**B:** Cut 1 ▢, 2" x 2", from *each*	**C:** Cut 1 ▭, 2" x 3½", from *each*

Circle of Friends

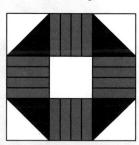 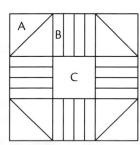 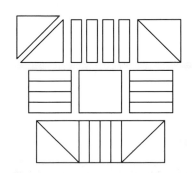

▢	**A:** Cut 2 ◺, 2⅞" x 2⅞"	**C:** Cut 1 ▭, 2½" x 2½"
■	**A:** Cut 2 ◺, 2⅞" x 2⅞"	
■■	**B:** Cut 8 ▭, 1" x 2½", from *each*	

Life

Notes from Mimi's Journal

Life can be like a crazy quilt. Each day and moment is unique: some are happy, some sad; some peaceful, some frustrating. The pieces are all different, but somehow they all fit together and life really is beautiful. Remember, if life gives you scraps—make a quilt!

Inspiration

- Celebrate the good moments in your life.
- Respect the challenging moments.
- Is your life a combination of "Light and Shadow"?
- Was there a "Broken Dishes" time in your life? You don't have to write about it, but remember it as you stitch a block.
- Is your life like a "Crazy Quilt"?

Key to My Diary

I made this block for my Diary quilt because . . .

_____

_____

_____

Crazy Quilt

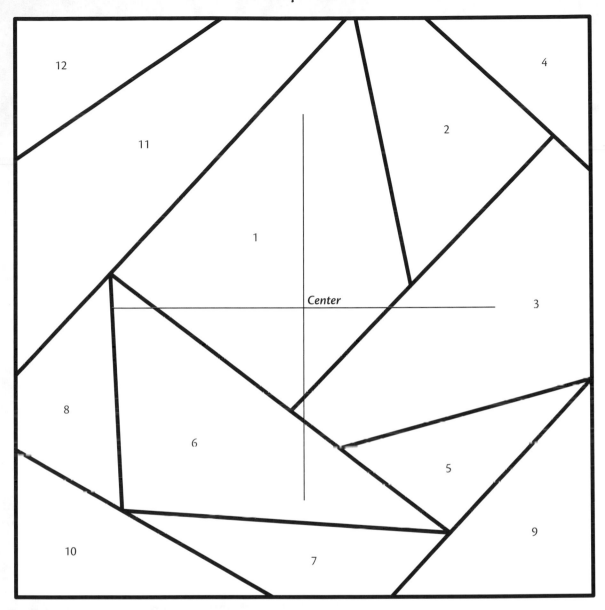

Trace the design onto a 6½" square of muslin.
Foundation piece the sections in numerical order.

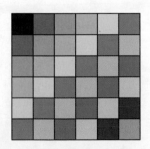

Sunshine
and Shadow

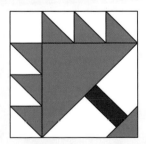

Tree of Life

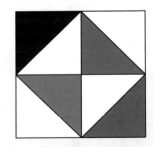

Broken Dishes

Broken Dishes

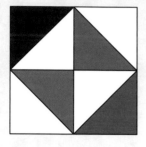 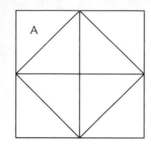 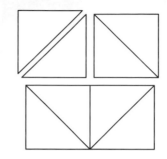

☐	**A:** Cut 2 ◻, 3⅞" x 3⅞"	
■■■■	**A:** Cut 1 ◻, 3⅞" x 3⅞", from *each* (1 left over of *each* color)	

Sunshine and Shadow

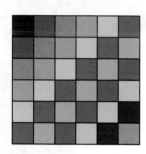 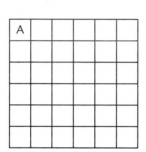 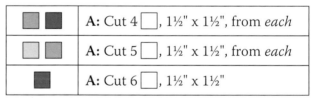

■ ■	**A:** Cut 1 ☐, 1½" x 1½", from *each*	
■ ■	**A:** Cut 2 ☐, 1½" x 1½", from *each*	
■ ■	**A:** Cut 3 ☐, 1½" x 1½", from *each*	

■ ■	**A:** Cut 4 ☐, 1½" x 1½", from *each*	
■ ■	**A:** Cut 5 ☐, 1½" x 1½", from *each*	
■	**A:** Cut 6 ☐, 1½" x 1½"	

Crosses and Losses

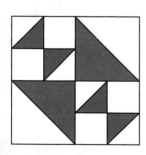 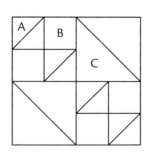 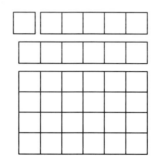 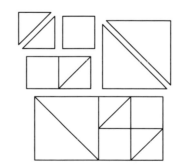

☐	**A:** Cut 2 ◻, 2⅜" x 2⅜"	**B:** Cut 4 ☐, 2" x 2"	**C:** Cut 1 ◻, 3⅞" x 3⅞"
■	**A:** Cut 2 ◻, 2⅜" x 2⅜"		
■	**C:** Cut 1 ◻, 3⅞" x 3⅞"		

Tree of Life

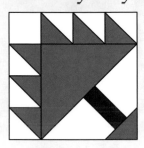 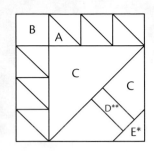 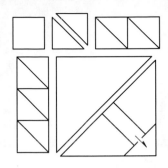

☐	**A:** Cut 3 ◣, 2⅜" x 2⅜"	**B:** Cut 1 ☐, 2" x 2"	**C:** Cut 1 ◩, 5⅜" x 5⅜" (1 left over)
◼	**A:** Cut 3 ◣, 2⅜" x 2⅜"	**E:** Cut 1 ◿, 2" x 2"*	**C:** Cut 1 ◩, 5⅜" x 5⅜" (1 left over)
◼	**D:** Cut 1 ▭, 1¼" x 2¾"**		

*Refer to page 117 to place E square in corner of white C triangle and sew on diagonal line to form small triangle.

**Turn under ¼" seam allowances on long edges and appliqué diagonally to white C triangle.

Light and Shadows

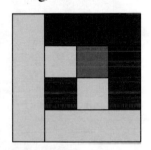 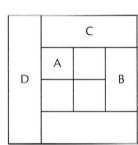 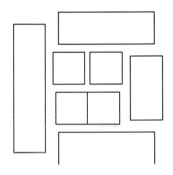

◼	**A:** Cut 1 ☐, 2" x 2"		
◼	**A:** Cut 1 ☐, 2" x 2"	**B:** Cut 1 ▭, 2" x 3½"	**C:** Cut 1 ▭, 2" x 5"
◻	**A:** Cut 2 ☐, 2" x 2"	**C:** Cut 1 ▭, 2" x 5"	**D:** Cut 1 ▭, 2" x 6½"

Storm at Sea

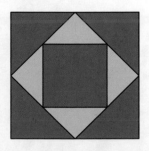 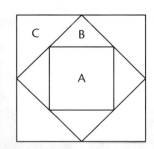 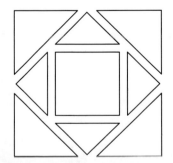

◼	**A:** Cut 1 ☐, 3½" x 3½"	**C:** Cut 2 ◩, 3⅞" x 3⅞"
◻	**B:** Cut 1 ⊠, 4¼" x 4¼"	

Retirement

Notes from Mimi's Journal

Celebrate! The "Evening Star" may be shining or the sand in the "Hourglass" may be falling, but retirement gives you time to enjoy life. Visit friends, play with grandchildren, take a trip you've always dreamed about, or just spend the morning quilting in your pajamas! Don't call me too early—I'll be sleeping late.

Inspiration

- What is your retirement dream?
- Will you move to the beach and wake to the sound of the "Ocean Waves" in the morning?
- Will you travel to a special place?
- Will you finish some of your quilting UFOs?
- Will you just enjoy the "Peace and Plenty" of the time?

Key to My Diary

I made this block for my Diary quilt because . . .

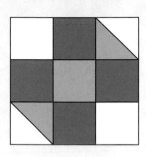

Hourglass

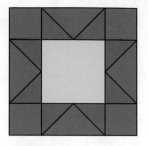

Evening Star

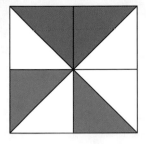

Peace and Plenty

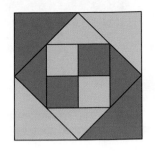

Ocean Wave

Super Stars

Center

Refer to page 8 to chain stitch the swirls.
Embellish the block with star-shaped buttons.

Evening Star

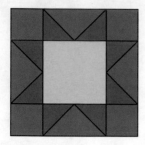 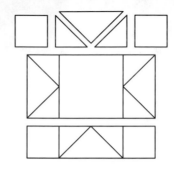

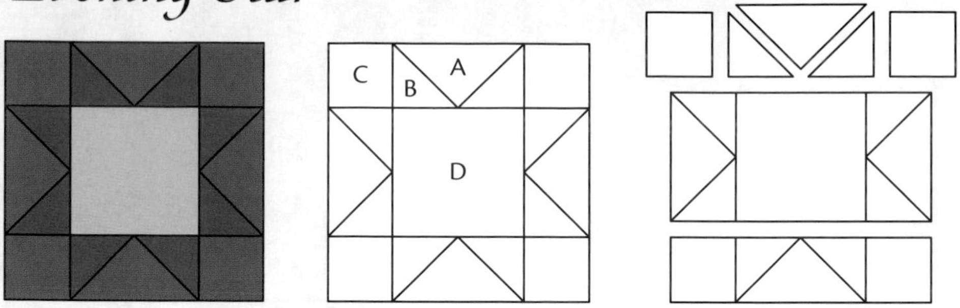

⬛	**A:** Cut 1 ⊠, 4¼" x 4¼"	**C:** Cut 4 ☐, 2" x 2"	
⬛	**B:** Cut 4 ◺, 2⅜" x 2⅜"		
⬛	**D:** Cut 1 ☐, 3½" x 3½"		

Footprints in the Sands of Time

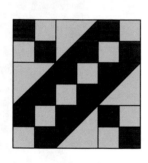 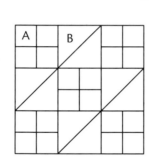 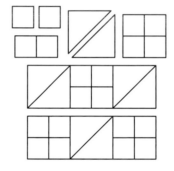

▨ ⬛	**A:** Cut 10 ☐, 1½" x 1½", from *each*	**B:** Cut 2 ◺, 2⅞" x 2⅞", from *each*

Hourglass

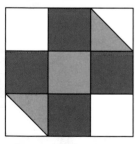 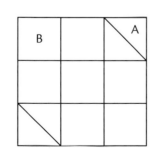 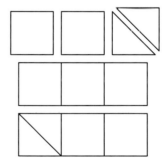

☐	**A:** Cut 1 ◺, 2⅞" x 2⅞"	**B:** Cut 2 ☐, 2½" x 2½"	
▨	**A:** Cut 1 ◺, 2⅞" x 2⅞"	**B:** Cut 1 ☐, 2½" x 2½"	
⬛	**B:** Cut 4 ☐, 2½" x 2½"		

Ocean Wave

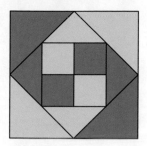 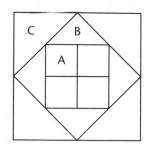 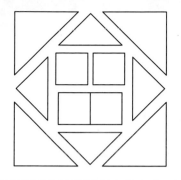

	A: Cut 2 ▢, 2" x 2", from *each*	**B:** Cut 1 ⊠, 4¼" x 4¼", from *each* (2 left over of *each* color)	**C:** Cut 1 ◺, 3⅞" x 3⅞", from *each*

Crossroads

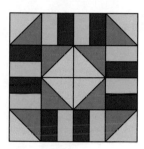 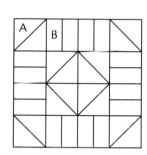 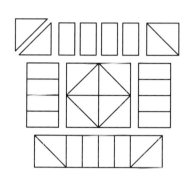

	A: Cut 4 ◺, 2⅜" x 2⅜", from *each*
	B: Cut 8 ▭, 1¼" x 2", from *each*

Peace and Plenty

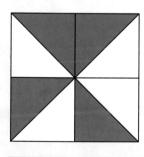 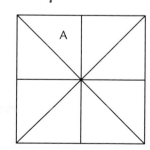 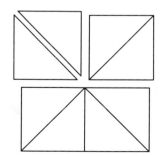

▢	**A:** Cut 2 ◺, 3⅞" x 3⅞"
▣ ▣	**A:** Cut 1 ◺, 3⅞" x 3⅞", from *each*

Dreams and Wishes

Notes from Mimi's Journal

I'm always dreaming. I like to ask myself "what if . . . ?" and then see what happens when I take a chance and act upon it. You never know what will come about when you make a wish, dare to dream, take a leap of faith, and attempt to make things happen. These are adventures.

Inspiration

- Do you have "Bright Hopes" for a project?
- Do you dream of "Sailing Away"?
- Do you make wishes on "Fireflies" in the summertime?
- Do you love finding "Four-Leaf Clovers"?
- Write down your dreams and wishes and put them into the Envelope block. They might come true!

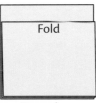

Key to My Diary

I made this block for my Diary quilt because . . .

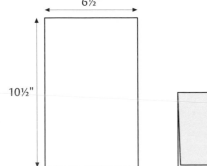

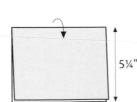

Make a secret envelope block to store the "Key" to your Diary quilt.

1. Cut a 6½" x 6½" background square.

2. Cut a 6½" x 10½" rectangle for the "pocket." Fold the rectangle, wrong sides together, so it measures 5¼" x 6½".

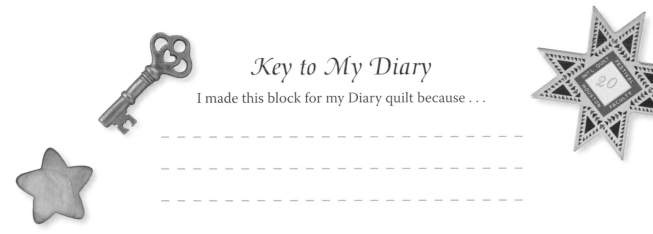

6½"

10½"

5¼"

3. Place the pocket so the raw edges match the bottom edge of the background square.

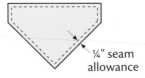

Fold

Raw edges

4. Cut two envelope flaps, adding ¼" seam allowance to all edges.

¼" seam allowance

Secret Envelope Block

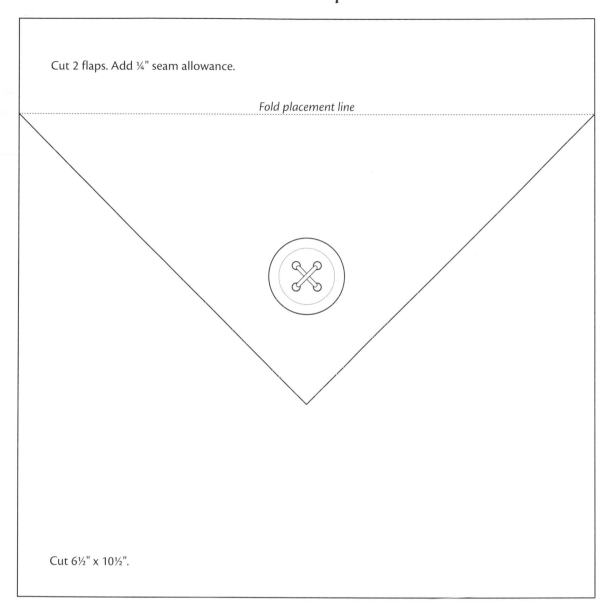

Cut 2 flaps. Add ¼" seam allowance.

Fold placement line

Cut 6½" x 10½".

5. Sew the flaps, right sides together, leaving the top straight edge open. Turn the flap right side out and place it over the pocket with the raw edges matching the top edge of the background square.

6. Use a button, snap, or hook-and-loop tape to secure the pocket flap.

Raw edges

Sail Away

Bright Hopes

Sail Away

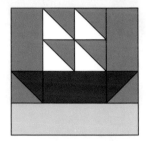 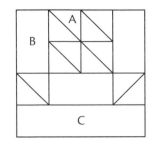 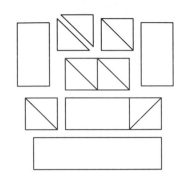

⬜	**A:** Cut 2 �« , 2⅜" x 2⅜"				
🟦	**A:** Cut 3 �« , 2⅜" x 2⅜"	**B:** Cut 2 ▭ , 2" x 3½"			
⬛	**A:** Cut 1 �« , 2⅜" x 2⅜"	**B:** Cut 1 ▭ , 2" x 3½"			
🟨	**C:** Cut 1 ▭ , 2" x 6½"				

Fireflies

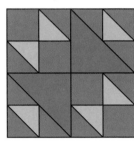 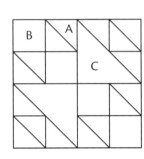 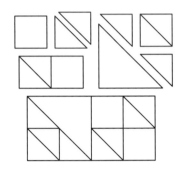

🟦	**A:** Cut 5 �« , 2⅜" x 2⅜"	**B:** Cut 4 ▭ , 2" x 2"	
🟩	**A:** Cut 3 ◣ , 2⅜" x 2⅜"		
🟦	**C:** Cut 1 ◣ , 3⅞" x 3⅞"		

Four-Leaf Clover

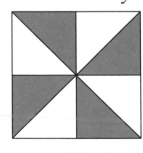 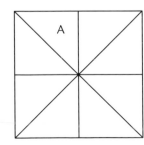 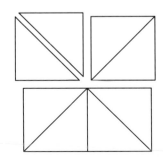

⬜ 🟩	**A:** Cut 2 ◣ , 3⅞" x 3⅞", from *each*

Wishing Ring

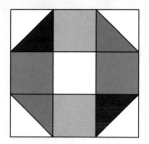

☐	**A:** Cut 2 ◸, 2⅞" x 2⅞"	**B:** Cut 1 ☐, 2½" x 2½"
◾ ◾	**B:** Cut 2 ☐, 2½" x 2½", from *each*	
◾ ◾	**A:** Cut 1 ◿, 2⅞" x 2⅞", from *each*	

Bright Hopes

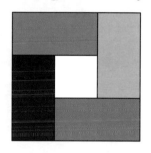 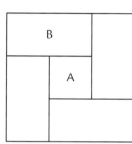 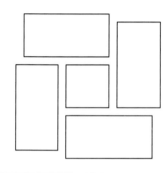

☐	**A:** Cut 1 ☐, 2½" x 2½"
◾ ◾ ◾ ◾	**B:** Cut 1 ▭, 2½" x 4½", from *each*

Dream Weaver

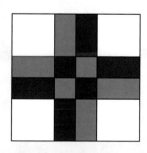 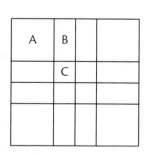 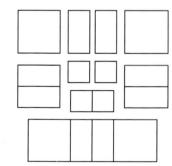

☐	**A:** Cut 4 ☐, 2½" x 2½"	
◾ ◾	**B:** Cut 4 ▭, 1½" x 2½", from *each*	**C:** Cut 2 ☐, 1½" x 1½", from *each*

Legacy

Notes from Mimi's Journal

When I made my first quilt, I learned that my great-grandmother had also been a quiltmaker. I was fascinated by the fact that she had stitched entire quilts by hand. Although I never knew her, I knew that her hands touched the same quilts that I held in my hands. I want my great-grandchildren to touch my quilts. I want them to feel the connections and remember me.

"There are truthfully messages that are stitched into those quilts. And sometimes they are messages of joy and sometimes they are messages of sorrow. Sometimes they are messages of hope and sometimes they are messages of desperation. But I think there's one message that's always stitched in, and it is: Don't forget me. I was here. Remember me.

Remember me."

—Karey Bresenhan, speaking about antique quilts in the film The Great American Quilt Revival, Bonesteel Films Inc., 2005.

Inspiration

- ❧ Have you ever touched an antique quilt made by a family member?

- ❧ Have you ever felt a connection to a quilt in a museum?

- ❧ How do you want your children and grandchildren to remember you?

- ❧ What do you want future generations to know about you?

- ❧ Is there one word that describes you?

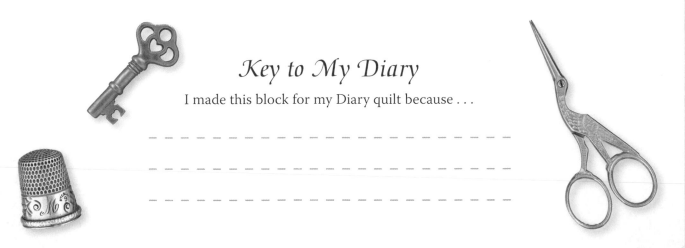

Key to My Diary

I made this block for my Diary quilt because . . .

- -

- -

- -

Remember Me

When this you see,
Remember me

Center

Refer to page 8 to chain stitch the words. You can also trace
the words with a fine-point permanent pen—or crayons!

"Memory Quilt" by Pamela Budesheim.
Pamela embellished the Ocean Waves block
with a cute whale button.

"My Quilting Life" by Norma Campbell. Norma loves '30s fabrics and uses them in many of the quilts she makes. The blocks in her Quilter's Diary were selected from some of her favorite quilts.

"*Threads of Time: A Family History*" by Lynn Irwin. Lynn's quilt setting is unusual. Look closely on the right side for paw prints. The shamrocks reflect Lynn's heritage.

"Mother's Life" by Genie Corbin.
The center of her quilt represents
Genie's family, with the musical instruments
representing her two sons.

"Quilted Memories" by Fran Timmins.
Fran broke her leg. That's why Sunbonnet Sue
has crutches and a cast on her foot.

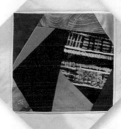

"Celebración" by Alice Isenbart.
Alice sees her life as a shining star,
and her quilt setting is amazing! The
bright colors reflect her Hispanic heritage.

"It's All About Me" by Elaine Loughlin.
Elaine outlined the white glove with blue
embroidery stitches to make it stand out
against the light background fabric.

"Life of Joy" by Eleanor Eckman.
Eleanor's bright colors are joyful. Her favorite block
is Grandmother's Flower Garden, representing quilts
made by her grandmother, her mother, and herself.

"Life's Memories" by Vera Hall.
Vera's embroidery blocks are her favorites.
As a child, Vera spent many hours with
her Aunt Elvie, learning to sew.

"Once Upon a Time"
by Barb Kopf.
Barb used
international
maritime flags
to represent the
first letters of her
grandsons' names.

"Nee Nee's Story Quilt"
by Millie Tracey.
Millie made this quilt
for her grandchildren.
Her granddaughter
loves to hear Nee Nee
tell the stories
in the blocks.

"Memories" by Kathy Stackhouse.
Kathy's Best Friend block is for her husband, who
is truly her best friend. Kathy shows her love for
patchwork blocks in this color-coordinated diary.

"A Few of my Favorite Things" by Kay Worley.
Kay fussy cut her favorite things from her fabric collection
and appliquéd them to a printed background. Kay might
inspire you to use your fabric stash to tell your story.

Basic Quiltmaking

If you bought this book, I'm sure you are a quilter! I have included basic techniques for cutting and piecing your blocks, as well as for assembling your quilt top. If you need more detailed quilting information, look through your favorite quilting books or check with the staff of your favorite quilt shop.

Rotary Cutting

It's easy to cut patchwork pieces with a rotary cutter, mat, and acrylic ruler. The symbols under the patchwork blocks refer to pieces that are rotary cut: squares, rectangles, half-square triangles, and quarter-square triangles.

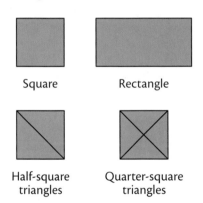

Square   Rectangle

Half-square triangles   Quarter-square triangles

The measurements printed with the symbols refer to the cut size of the piece and include ¼" seam allowances for sewing the pieces together. Do not add seam allowances to these pieces.

Cutting Squares and Rectangles

When you see the ☐ or ▭ symbol, cut a strip of fabric the measurement of the square or the smallest measurement of the rectangle.

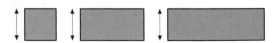

To cut squares and rectangles, cut across the strip according to the measurement of the square or the longer measurement of the rectangle.

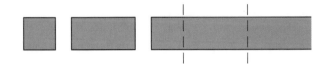

If you are designing your own patchwork block with squares or rectangles, add ½" to the finished measurements of these shapes for seam allowances.

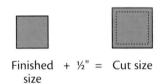

Finished + ½" = Cut size
size

Cutting Half-Square Triangles

When you see the ◻ symbol, cut a square the size of the given measurement. Cut the square diagonally from corner to corner in one direction to yield two half-square triangles. If this quick-cutting technique yields more pieces than you need, save the extras for another project.

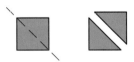

If you are designing your own patchwork block with half-square triangles, add ⅞" to the finished measurement of the short side of the triangle for seam allowances.

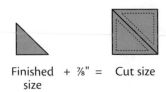

Finished + ⅞" = Cut size
size

Cutting Quarter-Square Triangles

When you see the ⊠ symbol, cut a square the size of the given measurement. Cut the square diagonally from corner to corner in both directions to yield four quarter-square triangles. If this quick-cutting technique yields more pieces than you need, save the extras for another project.

If you are designing your own patchwork block with quarter-square triangles, add 1¼" to the finished measurement of the long side of the triangle for seam allowances.

Finished + 1¼" = Cut size
size

Quick Corner Triangles

Pieces marked with this symbol ◻ refer to small squares sewn diagonally onto corners of larger squares or rectangles to create quick-and-easy triangles. The dimensions for these pieces will be followed by an asterisk, and the corresponding note, along with the block illustration, will indicate where to place these squares.

1. Draw a diagonal line on the wrong side of the small square.

2. Place the small square in the corner of the larger piece with the marked diagonal line following the same direction shown in the block diagram.

3. Sew on the diagonal line, and then press the piece out toward the corner to make the triangle. Trim the two layers underneath, leaving a ¼" seam allowance.

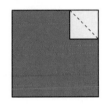

Piecing the Blocks

Once you've cut all the pieces, it's time to sew them together. Each block design in the book includes a piecing diagram that shows the pieces separately and gives you a picture of how they fit together. Whenever possible, sew the pieces together into squares using ¼"-wide seam allowances.

Then sew the squares into rows.

Then sew the rows into blocks.

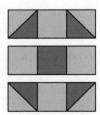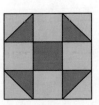

Appliquéing Basics

There are many appliqué methods. The following basic techniques are my favorites.

Cutting and Marking the Background Fabric

Cut the background fabric for the appliqué blocks 6½" square. Sometimes when I appliqué, I cut the blocks 1" larger and then trim them to the correct size when I am ready to put the quilt together.

To accurately position the appliqué pieces on the background fabric, mark the design directly on the fabric. Use a fabric marking pencil or a water-erasable marker to trace the design exactly on the lines.

If you are making a quilt with straight-set blocks, fold your background fabric into quarters by folding the square in half horizontally and verti-cally. Place the background fabric right side up over the pattern. Place the folds on the red lines marked on each pattern, matching the center of the design. Tape your fabric over the pattern using removable tape, and trace.

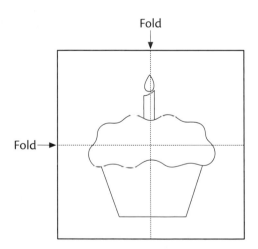

If you are making a quilt with the blocks on point, fold the fabric in half *diagonally* in both directions. Place the folds on the red lines marked on each pattern, matching the center of the design. Tape your fabric over the pattern using removable tape, and trace.

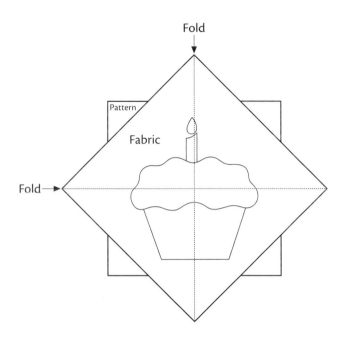

Making the Appliqué Templates

My favorite appliqué technique uses freezer-paper templates to shape the pieces and prepare them for appliqué. Of course, you can use another method if you prefer.

1. Place a piece of freezer paper, coated side down, over the appliqué design and trace each indi-vidual shape onto the uncoated side with a fine-lead mechanical pencil. Leave a small amount of space between each shape.

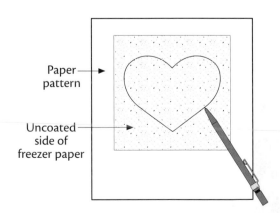

2. Cut out the freezer-paper templates on the traced lines so that they are exactly the same size as the finished pieces.

3. With the coated side down, iron the freezer-paper templates onto the wrong side of the appropriate fabrics, leaving at least ½" between pieces that will be cut from the same fabric. Press, using a warm, dry iron. Let the pieces cool.

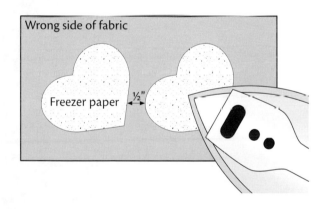

Wrong side of fabric

Freezer paper   ½"

4. Cut out the appliqué pieces, adding a ¼" seam allowance of fabric around the outside edge of each piece.

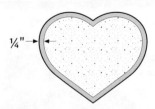

¼"

5. For each piece, turn the ¼" seam allowance toward the freezer paper and baste it in place by hand or use a glue stick to baste it to the paper.

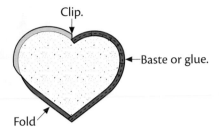

Clip.

Baste or glue.

Fold

6. Pin or baste the first piece to the background fabric. Appliqué it in place using the traditional appliqué stitch (see "The Appliqué Stitch" on page 120).

7. When you have stitched the appliqué in place, remove the basting stitches or pins. Cut a small slit in the background fabric behind the appliqué piece and remove the freezer paper.

8. Repeat steps 6 and 7 with the remaining appliqués, working in numerical order.

The Appliqué Stitch

1. Thread your needle with a single strand of thread that matches the color of the appliqué piece. Cut it approximately 18" long and tie a knot in one end.

2. To begin, slip the needle into the seam allowance from the wrong side of the appliqué piece, bringing it out along the folded edge. The knot will be hidden inside the seam allowance.

3. Stitch along the outer edge of the appliqué piece. Insert the needle into the background fabric, directly opposite where the thread came out of the seam allowance.

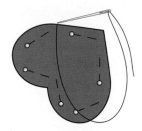

4. Let the needle travel along the background fabric, parallel to the edge of the appliqué, bringing it up about ⅛" from the last stitch.

As you bring the needle back up, pierce the edge of the appliqué piece, catching only one or two threads of the folded edge.

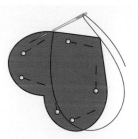

5. Move your needle straight off of the appliqué edge and back into the background fabric. Let your needle travel under the background, bringing it up ⅛" from the last stitch, again catching the edge of the appliqué. Give the thread a slight tug and continue stitching in this manner around the appliqué piece. Tie a knot on the back when you are finished.

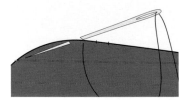

Assembling the Quilt Top

Before you assemble the blocks, trim each one to a perfect 6½" square, keeping the design centered. You can assemble the blocks in straight or diagonal settings.

Straight Settings

For straight settings, lay out the blocks on a flat surface. Sew the blocks together into rows; then join the rows to complete the center of the quilt.

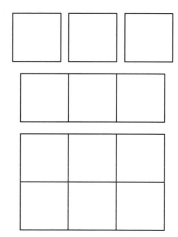

Straight Settings with Sashing Strips

1. Lay out the blocks on a flat surface.

2. Cut the inner vertical sashing strips 1½" x 6½" and place them between the blocks.

3. Sew the blocks and strips together into rows.

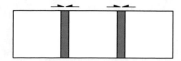

4. Cut the inner horizontal setting strips 1½" x the measurement of the pieced rows. Or, if sashing squares are part of the horizontal rows, sew them into long rows with the sashing pieces.

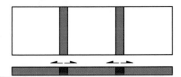

5. Sew the rows together with the horizontal sashing strips.

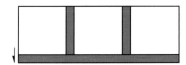

Diagonal Settings

For a diagonal setting, arrange and construct the quilt in diagonal rows, adding setting triangles around the edges to complete the corners and sides of the quilt. Lay out all the blocks and setting triangles on a flat surface before you start sewing. Pick up and sew one diagonal row at a time, and then join the rows to complete the quilt top.

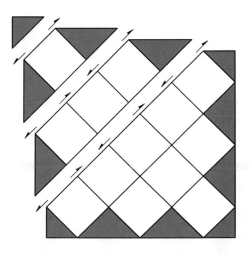

Adding Borders

After you have sewn the blocks together, the borders add a finishing frame to your design. A narrow 1"-wide inner border will nicely accent your blocks. If you have an "inspiration" fabric, it will make the perfect outer border for your quilt.

When you are ready to add the borders, cut them to match the size of your quilt. Check the size by measuring the quilt top through the center. Sometimes the edges of the quilt stretch, and a measurement of the center will be accurate and help you avoid distorted borders. Cut the borders according to the center measurements of the quilt. This step is very important!

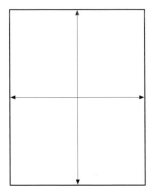

Measure center of quilt.

Overlapped borders are easy to apply. Two of the border strips are cut to the size of the inner quilt design; the other two borders are cut longer, to the total size of the quilt.

1. Measure the quilt top through the vertical center and cut two side border strips to this length. Fold the quilt in half horizontally and mark the quilt edges at the side center point with a pin. Fold each border strip in half crosswise and mark the center fold with a pin. Match the center of each side border strip to the center of your quilt and pin them together, easing the edge of the quilt to fit the borders.

2. Sew the side borders to the quilt. Press the seam allowances toward the border.

3. Measure the quilt top through the horizontal center, including the borders you just added. Cut two border strips to this length. Pin, and then sew the border strips to the top and bottom edges of the quilt top in the same manner as for the side borders. Press the seam allowances toward the border.

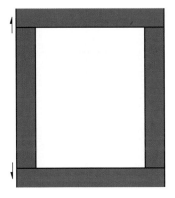

Signing Your Quilt

In the 1990s, I examined quilts from the textile collection of the Smithsonian Institution. The quilts are fabulous! The colors, fabrics, and stitches are incredible. But I came home wanting to know more. Who were the quilters? Why did they make quilts? Where did they live? Why did they choose their fabrics? These questions might have had more answers if the quilters had signed their quilts.

Many quilters sign their creations or sew a label to the back of their quilts. If you want a complete "Key to Your Diary," you can make a larger label (see the quilt label on the back of my Diary quilt on page 124). Sew it to the back of your quilt or place it in a fabric envelope.

Make sure you include your name, the date, and the place where you live. Add a dedication and the names of the quilt blocks you used. If you wish, write a story to explain your choices. Give your family some clues to the secrets in the stitches. Your family will love you for it, and I'm sure they will be fascinated. They will remember you!

Signatures

Your own handwriting is the perfect way to sign your quilt. Your signature is unique and will add a personal touch to your Diary quilt story. Write directly on the fabric with a fine-point permanent pen. Sign a block on the front of your quilt, write on the back of your quilt, or make a label to stitch to the back. You can also use an extra patchwork block for a signature block and stitch it to the back of the quilt.

Computer-Generated Labels

Use a computer to print the information you want and trace it onto fabric with a fine-point permanent pen to make the label for your quilt. You can also print the information directly onto specially prepared fabric for your computer.

Appliquéd Monogram

Use your monogram to sign your quilt with a personal touch. I photocopied my monogram from a favorite tote bag that was monogrammed at a shop in a mall. You can create your own monogram with letters and fancy fonts on your computer. Print them out and enlarge them to make them fit into a 6" square. Appliqué the letters using Ultrasuede or wool—you don't have to turn under the edges.

Signal Flags

Some of my students have used signal flags to sign their quilts, add initials of grandchildren, and even convey secret messages. Don't they look like patchwork blocks?

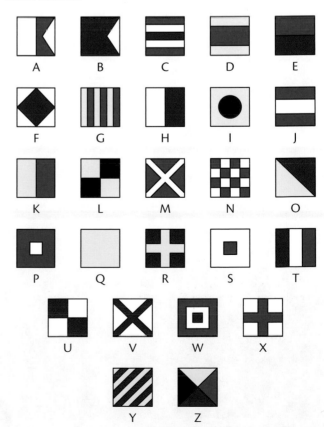

Mimi's Label

This is the label from my Diary quilt, shown on the facing page. To print on fabric I used a product called Printed Treasures. To find the blocks, think of the quilt in the photo at right like a bingo card—letters across the top and numbers going down. For instance, Sunbonnet Sue is D3. You'll be able to find the blocks!

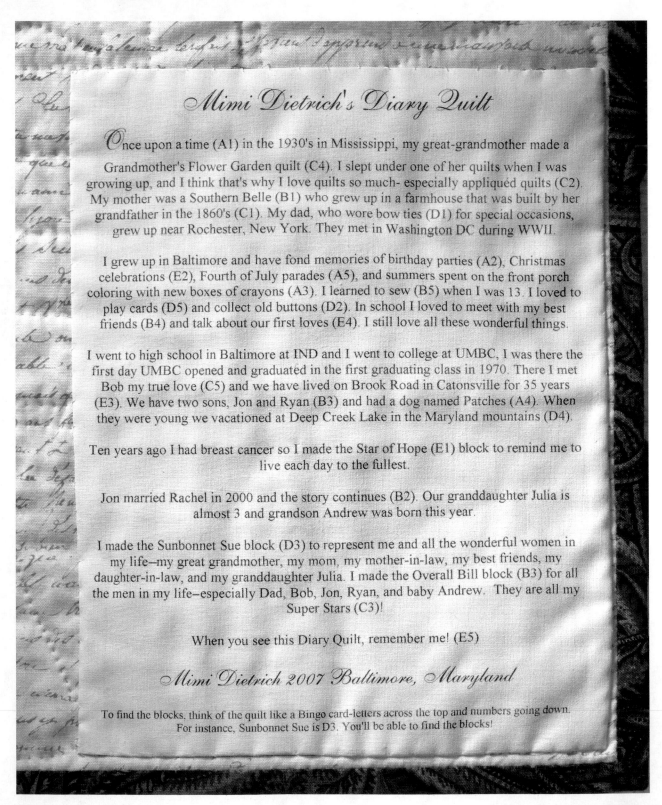

Mimi Dietrich's Diary Quilt

Once upon a time (A1) in the 1930's in Mississippi, my great-grandmother made a Grandmother's Flower Garden quilt (C4). I slept under one of her quilts when I was growing up, and I think that's why I love quilts so much- especially appliquéd quilts (C2). My mother was a Southern Belle (B1) who grew up in a farmhouse that was built by her grandfather in the 1860's (C1). My dad, who wore bow ties (D1) for special occasions, grew up near Rochester, New York. They met in Washington DC during WWII.

I grew up in Baltimore and have fond memories of birthday parties (A2), Christmas celebrations (E2), Fourth of July parades (A5), and summers spent on the front porch coloring with new boxes of crayons (A3). I learned to sew (B5) when I was 13. I loved to play cards (D5) and collect old buttons (D2). In school I loved to meet with my best friends (B4) and talk about our first loves (E4). I still love all these wonderful things.

I went to high school in Baltimore at IND and I went to college at UMBC, I was there the first day UMBC opened and graduated in the first graduating class in 1970. There I met Bob my true love (C5) and we have lived on Brook Road in Catonsville for 35 years (E3). We have two sons, Jon and Ryan (B3) and had a dog named Patches (A4). When they were young we vacationed at Deep Creek Lake in the Maryland mountains (D4).

Ten years ago I had breast cancer so I made the Star of Hope (E1) block to remind me to live each day to the fullest.

Jon married Rachel in 2000 and the story continues (B2). Our granddaughter Julia is almost 3 and grandson Andrew was born this year.

I made the Sunbonnet Sue block (D3) to represent me and all the wonderful women in my life—my great grandmother, my mom, my mother-in-law, my best friends, my daughter-in-law, and my granddaughter Julia. I made the Overall Bill block (B3) for all the men in my life—especially Dad, Bob, Jon, Ryan, and baby Andrew. They are all my Super Stars (C3)!

When you see this Diary Quilt, remember me! (E5)

Mimi Dietrich 2007 Baltimore, Maryland

To find the blocks, think of the quilt like a Bingo card-letters across the top and numbers going down. For instance, Sunbonnet Sue is D3. You'll be able to find the blocks!

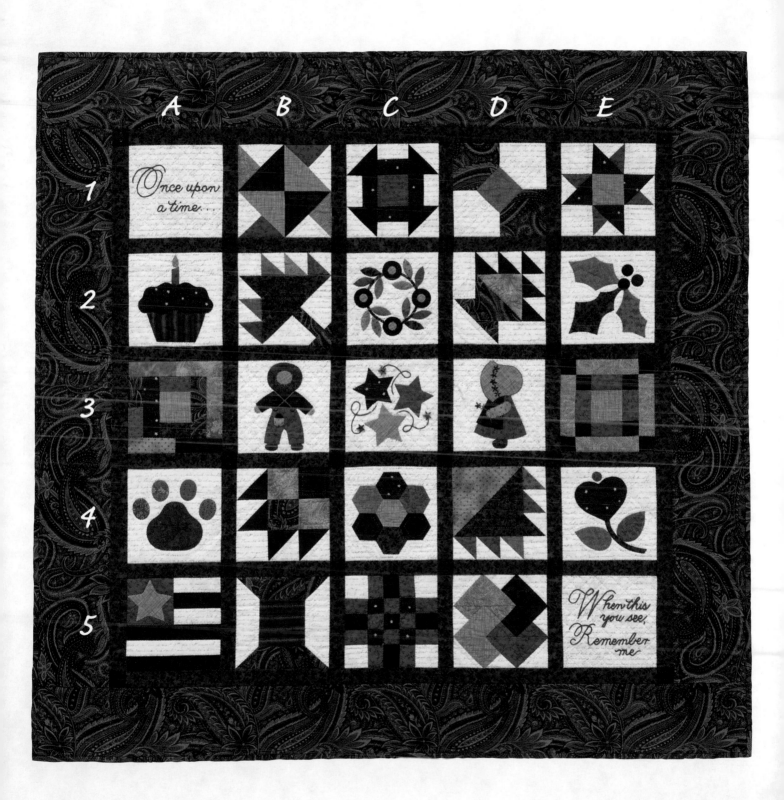

Bibliography

Quilt Blocks

Better Homes and Gardens Books. *501 Quilt Blocks.* Des Moines, IA: Meredith Corporation, 1994.

BlockBase. CD-ROM. The Electric Quilt Company, 1991-2000.

Brackman, Barbara. *Encyclopedia of Pieced Quilt Patterns.* Paducah, KY: American Quilter's Society, 1993.

Gordon, Maggi McCormick. *1000 Great Quilt Blocks.* Woodinville, WA: Martingale & Company, 2003.

Hopkins, Judy. *Around the Block.* Woodinville, WA: Martingale & Company, 1994.

Kratovil, Debby. *Quilter's Block-a-Day Calendar.* Woodinville, WA: Martingale & Company, 2007.

Malone, Maggie. *5500 Quilt Block Designs.* New York, NY: Sterling Publishing Company, 2003.

Martin, Nancy. *365 Quilt Blocks a Year.* Woodinville, WA: Martingale & Company, 1999.

Basic Quiltmaking

Doak, Carol. *Your First Quilt Book (or it should be!).* Woodinville, WA: Martingale & Company, 1997

Appliqué

Dietrich, Mimi. *Baltimore Basics: Album Quilts from Start to Finish.* Woodinville, WA: Martingale & Company, 2006.

———. *Mimi Dietrich's Favorite Appliqué Quilts.* Woodinville, WA: Martingale & Company, 2007.

Finishing Your Quilt

Dietrich, Mimi. *Happy Endings: Finishing the Edges of Your Quilt,* rev. ed. Woodinville, WA: Martingale & Company, 2003.